MEAT

CLASSIC CHEESEBURGER

WITH HOMEMADE PICKLES

1½ lb./680 g freshly ground/
    minced beef, 20% fat
4 slices Cheddar cheese
4 hamburger buns
kosher salt and cracked black pepper
oil, for brushing the grate

HOMEMADE PICKLES
6 Persian cucumbers, sliced into rounds
2 bay leaves
2 cups/500 ml white wine vinegar
½ cup/110 g white sugar
2 tablespoons kosher salt
2 teaspoons mustard seeds

TO SERVE
sliced lettuce, sliced onions,
    sliced tomatoes, ketchup, and mayo

SERVES 4

A weekend barbecue is not complete without a classic hamburger. Use high-quality beef that has a good amount of fat in it—that way you will end up with a juicy mouthwatering burger. Homemade pickles add a nice tart crunch. Serve with a large platter piled high with lettuce, tomatoes, and onions and your guests can build their own burger.

Make the pickles ahead of time as they will need to marinate for at least an hour.

Pack the cucumbers and bay leaves into a sterilized glass jar. Bring the vinegar, sugar, salt, mustard seeds, and ¼ cup/ 60 ml water to the boil in a saucepan over medium–high heat. Reduce to a simmer and cook for 5 minutes until the sugar has dissolved. Pour the hot mixture over the cucumbers and bay leaves, cap with a tight-fitting lid, and set aside. These will keep for up to 6 months in the fridge.

Place the beef in a bowl, season with salt and pepper, and mix to combine. Gently shape the meat into four patties about 1 inch/2.5 cm thick. Using your thumb, gently make a small indentation in the center of each patty. This ensures they will keep their shape when cooking.

Heat a grill/barbecue to medium-high. Brush the grate with oil.

Place the patties on the grill and cook for 5 minutes. Flip them over and continue to cook for another 5 minutes for medium-rare, or longer for well done. For the last 2 minutes of cooking, place a slice of cheese on top of each patty to melt.

Slice the hamburger buns, toast them on the grill, then add the patties and pickles, and serve with lettuce, onions, tomatoes, ketchup, and mayo.

LAMB SMASH BURGERS

1½ lb./680 g freshly ground/
  minced lamb
1 tablespoon dried mint
1 tablespoon dried oregano
1 teaspoon pressed garlic
4 brioche burger buns or bread
  of your choice
4 thick tomato slices
sea salt and cracked black pepper
crumbled feta cheese, to serve
oil, for brushing the grate

AIOLI
2 egg yolks
1 garlic clove
½ teaspoon Dijon mustard
2 tablespoons freshly squeezed
  lemon juice
1 cup/240 ml extra virgin olive oil
2¼ cups/225 g pitted/stoned Kalamata
  olives, finely chopped

SERVES 4

Smash burgers are—as the name implies—smashed burgers! The key to success is to cook them in a searing-hot cast-iron pan and press the meat down into a flat patty, cooking until they have a crisp crust, then flip them over to cook the other side.

Place the lamb, mint, oregano, and garlic in a large bowl, season with salt and pepper, then stir to combine.

Divide the mixture into four and form into loose balls. Don't squeeze too hard as you want the mixture to be loose to smash down easily during cooking. Cover and set aside.

To make the aïoli, combine the egg yolks, garlic, mustard, and lemon juice in a food processor and process until smooth. With the motor running, slowly add in the olive oil, a few drops at a time. As the mixture thickens, continue to add the oil in a slow, steady stream until it is all combined. Transfer the aïoli into a bowl and stir in the chopped Kalamata olives.

Heat the grill/barbecue to medium–high. Brush the grate with oil.

Place a cast-iron pan or flat-top griddle on top and heat until smoking. Place the patties in the hot pan and firmly smash down with a flat spatula until they are ½ inch/1 cm thick.

Cook for about 2 minutes until a crisp crust forms. Flip them over and continue to cook for another minute for medium-rare, or longer for well done.

Slice the buns and toast them on the grill, then spread the top and bottom with a thick layer of aïoli. Place a patty on each bun base, then top with a tomato slice and sprinkle with feta cheese.

JERK PORK CHOPS

WITH MANGO SALSA & GRILLED PLANTAINS

4 bone-in pork chops
4 Habanero or Scotch Bonnet
  chiles/chillies
2-inch/5-cm piece of fresh ginger,
  peeled and roughly chopped
4 garlic cloves, peeled and smashed
1 tablespoon ground cinnamon
1 tablespoon ground allspice
1 tablespoon ground nutmeg
3 tablespoons molasses
sea salt
oil, for brushing the grate

MANGO SALSA
1 large fresh mango, peeled,
  pitted/stoned, and diced
1 shallot, finely minced
1 jalapeño chile/chilli, finely diced
small bunch of cilantro/coriander,
  chopped
grated zest and freshly squeezed
  juice of 1 large lime
2 tablespoons olive oil

GRILLED PLANTAINS
4 plantains, peeled and cut in half
  lengthwise
2 tablespoons olive oil
4 tablespoons honey

SERVES 4

A medley of flavors play out here, hot and spicy contrasting with cooling fruits. Grilled plantains are a mainstay of Caribbean cooking and are sweet and delicious. Serve with plain rice and ice-cold beers.

Place the pork chops in a ceramic dish large enough for them to lie in a single layer.

Place the chiles/chillies, ginger, garlic, cinnamon, allspice, nutmeg, molasses, and a good pinch of salt in a blender, and process to a coarse purée. Pour the marinade over the pork and toss to make sure the meat is completely covered. Cover and refrigerate for 6-24 hours.

To make the salsa, mix the mango, shallot, jalapeño, cilantro/coriander, lime zest and juice, and oil in a bowl. Cover and refrigerate until ready to use.

Remove the pork from the fridge and bring to room temperature.

Lay the plantains in a ceramic dish. Whisk together the oil and honey and pour over the plantains, making sure they are completely coated. Cover and set aside.

Heat the grill/barbecue to medium-high. Brush the grate with oil. Grill the pork chops for 6 minutes, then turn over. Reduce the heat slightly or move them to a cooler part of the grill and continue to cook for another 6-8 minutes. To check doneness, insert a sharp knife into the center of the chop—the juices should run clear and the meat be slightly pink. Remove to a plate, cover with foil, and rest for 10 minutes.

Place the plantains on the grill and cook for about 3-4 minutes on each side until dark golden brown and charred. Remove from the grill and serve with the pork chops and chilled mango salsa.

SMOKY HONEY CHIPOTLE RIBS

2 racks of baby-back pork ribs,
    membrane removed
1 cup/225 g fig jam
1 cup/240 ml dark honey
7-oz/198-g can of chipotle chiles/
    chillies in adobo sauce
1 Habanero chile/chilli
1 yellow onion, roughly chopped
4 garlic cloves, peeled and bashed
3-inch/7.5-cm piece of fresh ginger,
    peeled and roughly chopped
1 lime, quartered
1½ cups/75 g cilantro/coriander,
    roughly chopped
1 teaspoon sea salt
½ teaspoon cracked black pepper
oil, for brushing the grate

SERVES 6-8

Everyone loves ribs and baby-back pork ribs can take on powerful smoky flavor and spices. Marinating them overnight makes sure all the flavors soak into the meat. The ribs should cook over a low indirect heat for as long as possible to ensure the meat is tender and falling off the bones.

Place the ribs in a baking dish large enough to hold them in one layer.

Place all the remaining ingredients in a blender and process until you have a smooth sauce. Pour the sauce over the ribs, making sure they are completely coated. Cover and refrigerate for 6-24 hours.

When you are ready to cook, remove the ribs from the fridge and bring to room temperature.

Prepare a grill/barbecue for medium-low indirect heat (325-350°F/ 160-180°C)—this means lighting one side of the grill only. Brush the grate with oil. Place a small disposable foil pan filled with water over the heat—this will keep the ribs moist while cooking.

Using tongs, remove the ribs from the marinade and shake off any excess sauce. Reserve the leftover marinade for basting. Lay the ribs meat-side down on the grate away from the heat and close the lid. Cook for 1 hour.

After the first hour, turn the ribs over and baste with the reserved marinade sauce. Replenish the water in the foil pan and close the lid. Cook for another hour.

Baste the ribs one more time and close the lid for another 15 minutes.

Move the ribs over to the directly heated side of the grill and cook for 5 minutes, then turn the ribs over for another 5 minutes until browned and slightly charred.

Remove the ribs to a large wooden board and tent with foil. Rest for 10 minutes, then cut up and serve.

KOREAN GRILLED SKIRT STEAK

1 skirt steak, approx. 2 lb./900 g
Homemade Pickles (see page 29) and
    store-bought kimchi, to serve
oil, for brushing the grate

MARINADE
⅓ cup/80 ml vegetable oil
⅓ cup/80 ml soy sauce
⅓ cup/80 ml toasted sesame oil
⅓ cup/80 ml honey
3 tablespoons sherry
3 tablespoons curry powder
2 tablespoons freshly grated ginger
4 garlic cloves
sea salt and cracked black pepper

SERVES 4

Beautifully charred on the outside and ruby-red rare inside is how this steak comes off the hot coals. Served with Spicy Peanut Noodles (below), it's the perfect food for summer. Make quick Homemade Pickles (see page 29) to go alongside—you can also pickle a few green tomatoes too.

To make the marinade, place all the marinade ingredients in a blender and process to a smooth sauce. Season with salt and pepper.

Place the steak in a ceramic baking dish. Pour the marinade over the steak, turning the meat to make sure it is completely covered. Cover and refrigerate for 8–24 hours.

When you are ready to cook, remove the steak from the fridge and bring to room temperature.

Heat the grill/barbecue to medium-high. Brush the grate with oil.

Place the steak on the grill and cook for 5 minutes, then turn the steak over and cook for a further 5 minutes for medium-rare. Allow a longer time if you prefer the steak medium or well done.

Remove the steak from the grill, cover, and rest for 10 minutes.

Slice the steak against the grain and serve with Spicy Peanut Noodles, Homemade Pickles, and kimchi alongside.

SPICY PEANUT NOODLES

9-oz/250-g packet buckwheat soba noodles
⅓ cup/80 g doenjang (Korean bean paste)
⅓ cup/80 g gochujang (Korean chili/
    chilli paste)
cilantro/coriander, to garnish
sesame seeds, to garnish
4 limes, quartered, to serve

FOR THE SAUCE
2 tablespoons dark honey
2 tablespoons toasted sesame oil
½ yellow onion, roughly chopped
3 scallions/spring onions, roughly chopped
2 tablespoons peanut butter
2 tablespoons rice wine vinegar
sea salt and cracked black pepper

SERVES 4

These noodles are cloaked in a wonderful spicy peanut sauce, which can be served either ice-cold or warm. They make a great summer dish on their own, but are even better served with something caramelized and charred, hot off the grill. Keep the leftover sauce in a glass jar with a lid in the fridge and add a spoonful to dressings or mix into rice.

Cook the soba noodles according to the packet instructions. Rinse under cold water and set aside.

To make the sauce, place all the sauce ingredients in a blender and process until smooth. Season with salt and pepper.

Place the noodles in a large bowl and spoon over 2–3 tablespoons of the sauce. Toss together, making sure the noodles are well coated in the sauce. Sprinkle with cilantro/coriander and sesame seeds. Serve the limes on the side for squeezing over.

GRILLED STEAKS

WITH GRILLED TOMATILLO SALSA VERDE

6 New York strip/sirloin steaks
½ cup/120 ml olive oil
2 teaspoons smoked sea salt
2 teaspoons cracked black pepper
2 teaspoons chipotle chili/chilli powder
4 garlic cloves, finely minced
oil, for brushing the grate

SALSA VERDE
12 tomatillos, husks removed
1 yellow onion, cut into quarters
2 Serrano chiles/chillies
2 garlic cloves
small bunch of cilantro/coriander
freshly squeezed juice of 1 lime
sea salt and cracked black pepper

SERVES 6-8

Here New York strip steaks are used as this is a cut that grills really well, but you can use any type of steak, bone-in or boneless. Scorched and charred tomatillos make a wonderful salsa verde. Slice the steaks up on a big wooden board, generously spoon over the salsa verde, and serve with a big green crispy salad.

Place the steaks in a ceramic baking dish. In a small bowl, whisk together the oil, salt, pepper, chili/chilli powder, and garlic. Pour over the steaks, making sure both sides are coated. Cover and set aside.

Heat the grill/barbecue to medium-high. Brush the grate with oil.

To make the salsa verde, grill the tomatillos, onion, chiles/chillies, and garlic for about 5-6 minutes until they are cooked through and slightly charred. Transfer the vegetables to a blender, add the cilantro/coriander and lime juice, and process until you have a chunky sauce. Season with salt and pepper, pour into a bowl, and set aside.

Place the steaks on the grill and cook for 5 minutes, then turn them over and cook for a further 5 minutes for medium-rare. Allow a longer time if you prefer your steak medium or well done.

Remove the steaks from the grill to a wooden board, cover with foil, and rest for 10 minutes.

To serve, slice the steaks against the grain and spoon over the tomatillo salsa verde.

GRILLED LAMB

WITH NORTH AFRICAN SPICES & DATES

2 racks of lamb
1 tablespoon ground cardamom
1 tablespoon ground cumin
2 teaspoons chili/chilli powder
1 teaspoon ground cloves
1 teaspoon ground cinnamon
1 teaspoon ground allspice
1 teaspoon kosher salt
½ cup/120 ml date molasses
¼ cup/60 ml extra virgin olive oil
24 large dates, pitted/stoned
oil, for brushing the grate

HUMMUS
15-oz/440-g can of chickpeas, drained
2 tablespoons tahini
zest and freshly squeezed juice
    of 1 lemon
2 garlic cloves, peeled and bashed
¼ cup/60 ml extra virgin olive oil,
    plus extra for drizzling
sea salt and cracked black pepper
sumac, for sprinkling

SERVES 4

An explosion of wonderful spices laced with date molasses turns these lamb chops into one of the best things to come off a hot grill. As the dates cook on the hot fire, they caramelize and sweeten to a deep earthy taste. Served with an aromatic creamy hummus, it is perfect for long summer evenings with friends gathered around the grill.

Cut the lamb racks into single chops and place in a ceramic dish large enough to hold them.

In a bowl mix together the cardamom, cumin, chili/chilli powder, cloves, cinnamon, allspice, salt, date molasses, and olive oil. Pour over the lamb, making sure all the chops are completely covered. Cover and refrigerate for 4–24 hours.

Set aside 2 tablespoons of the chickpeas. Place the remainder of the chickpeas in the bowl of a food processor with the tahini, lemon zest and juice, garlic, and olive oil and pulse until smooth. Season with salt and pepper. Pour the hummus into a bowl, cover, and refrigerate.

Remove the lamb from the fridge and bring to room temperature.

Thread the dates onto skewers and set aside.

Remove the hummus from the fridge and top with the reserved chickpeas. Drizzle with olive oil and sprinkle with a little sumac.

Heat the grill/barbecue to medium-high. Brush the grate with oil.

Place the lamb chops on the grill and cook for 3–4 minutes. Using a pair of tongs, turn the chops over and continue to cook for another 3–4 minutes, or for longer if you prefer your meat well done. Remove the chops to a platter and tent with foil. Rest for 10 minutes.

Place the skewered dates on the grill and cook for 2–3 minutes until caramelized and slightly charred. Serve the chops with the dates and the hummus.

SRIRACHA & LIME GRILLED CHICKEN WINGS

24 chicken wings
¼ cup/60 ml sriracha
¼ cup/60 ml sambal oelek
¾ cup/180 ml dark runny honey
½ cup/125 ml toasted sesame oil
4 garlic cloves
2 makrut limes, or regular limes,
   quartered
6 makrut lime leaves, or regular
   lime leaves, shredded
1 small onion, roughly chopped
1 tablespoon black sesame seeds
sea salt and cracked black pepper
oil, for brushing the grate
tangerine wedges, to serve

SERVES 4-6

The fruit and leaves of the makrut lime tree add perfume and flavor to many dishes, but you can also use regular lime juice and leaves in this dish to add a pleasant, cooling contrast to all the spices. Chicken wings are a fun appetizer to hand around at a barbecue or to take to the beach for a picnic.

Rinse the chicken wings under running cold water and pat dry with paper towels. Place in a large ceramic dish or bowl.

Place the sriracha, sambal oelek, honey, sesame oil, garlic, lime quarters, lime leaves, and onion in a blender and process until you have a smooth sauce. Season with salt and pepper. Pour the sauce over the chicken wings and toss to coat. Cover and refrigerate for 4 hours or overnight.

When you are ready to cook, remove the chicken wings from the fridge and bring to room temperature.

Heat the grill/barbecue to medium-high. Brush the grate with oil.

Cook the wings on the grill for 6-8 minutes, then turn them over and either turn the heat down or move to a cooler part of the grill. Continue to cook for a further 8 minutes, turning occasionally to make sure they are cooked through and crispy on the outside.

Place the cooked wings on a large plate and sprinkle with the sesame seeds. Serve with the tangerine wedges.

GRILLED HARISSA CHICKEN KABOBS

12 chicken thighs, skin on, boneless
¼ cup/60 ml honey
oil, for brushing the grate
cracked green olives and lemon
    wedges, to serve

HARISSA
2 dried Pasilla chiles/chillies
1 dried Ancho chile/chilli
1 roasted red (bell) pepper
2 red Serrano chiles/chillies,
    roughly chopped
2 teaspoons ground cumin
2 tablespoons tomato paste/
    tomato purée
1 teaspoon smoked paprika
4 garlic cloves, peeled and bashed
2 tablespoons olive oil
½ teaspoon kosher salt

SERVES 6-8

This is one of my all-time favorite dishes to grill—spicy chicken, hot off the grill and served with lemon wedges and cracked green olives is divine. Serve with ice-cold beers and relax. Store the extra harissa in the fridge and use it to flavor stews, pastas, and grilled vegetables, or to spoon through rice dishes.

To make the harissa, place the dried Pasilla and Ancho chiles/chillies in a bowl, cover with boiling water, and soak for 30 minutes. Drain the chiles, reserving ¼ cup/60 ml of the soaking liquid.

Place the chiles, reserved liquid, and the remaining harissa ingredients in a blender and blend until you have a rough paste.

Place the chicken thighs in a large ceramic dish. Mix 4 tablespoons of the harissa paste with the honey. Pour over the chicken and toss to coat completely. Cover and refrigerate for 6–24 hours. (Pour the remaining harissa into a jar with a tight-fitting lid and refrigerate for up to 6 months.)

Remove the chicken from the fridge and thread onto metal skewers. Bring to room temperature.

Heat the grill/barbecue to medium–high. Brush the grate with oil.

Place the skewers skin-side down on the grill and cook for 8 minutes until golden brown and crispy. Turn the skewers over and turn down the heat or move to a cooler part of the grill. Continue to cook for another 15 minutes. Check for doneness by inserting a sharp knife into the chicken to see that the meat is no longer pink and the juices run clear.

Remove the cooked skewers from the grill, cover, and rest for 5 minutes.

Serve topped with the olives and lemon wedges (if you wish, the lemon wedges can be briefly charred on the grill).

CAJUN FRIED CHICKEN

4 lb./2 kg chicken, cut into 10 pieces
1½ cups/375 ml buttermilk
1 egg
1 cup/130 g all-purpose/plain flour
½ cup/75 g cornmeal/polenta
6 cups/1.4 litres vegetable oil,
    for deep-frying
sea salt and grated lemon zest,
    for sprinkling
lemon wedges and hot sauce, to serve

CAJUN SEASONING
2 teaspoons cumin
2 teaspoons cayenne
2 tablespoons Spanish smoked paprika
2 teaspoons dried oregano
1 teaspoon dried garlic powder
1 teaspoon sea salt
1 teaspoon cracked black pepper

SERVES 4-6

Fried chicken is a real summer dish especially suited to those long sunny days spent at the beach. Wrap it up for a picnic as it's as delicious eaten cold as hot. Generously sprinkle with lemon zest and sea salt for that extra tang and serve with an array of hot sauces.

To make the Cajun seasoning, mix all the ingredients together in a small bowl.

Place the chicken pieces in a large ceramic baking dish. In a bowl whisk together the buttermilk, egg, and 2 tablespoons of the Cajun seasoning. Pour over the chicken, making sure the pieces are evenly coated. Cover and refrigerate for 4–24 hours.

In a shallow bowl mix together the flour, cornmeal/polenta, and 1 tablespoon of the Cajun seasoning. (Store the remaining seasoning in an airtight container.)

Remove the chicken from the fridge and bring to room temperature.

Pour the oil into a 5-quart/5-litre Dutch oven or deep-fryer and heat until it registers 375°F/190°C on a deep-frying thermometer.

Remove the chicken from the buttermilk and shake off any excess marinade. Dredge each piece in the flour mix and, working in batches, fry the chicken in the hot oil for 8–10 minutes until dark golden brown and cooked through.

Remove the chicken pieces from the oil, drain on paper towels, and sprinkle with sea salt and lemon zest. Serve with lemon wedges and hot sauce of your choice.

PIRI PIRI CORNISH GAME HENS

WITH CITRUS-HONEY DIPPING SAUCE

2 Cornish game hens or poussins
6 hot red chiles/chillies, roughly
    chopped
2 teaspoons smoked paprika
4 garlic cloves, roughly chopped
grated zest and freshly squeezed juice
    of 1 lemon
½ cup/125 ml olive oil
sea salt and cracked black pepper
oil, for brushing the grate

CITRUS-HONEY DIPPING SAUCE
grated zest and freshly squeezed juice
    of 2 tangerines
2 tablespoons cider vinegar
2 tablespoons toasted sesame oil
2 tablespoons honey
1 teaspoon mirin
1 teaspoon fish sauce
½ Serrano chile/chilli, thinly sliced

SERVES 4

If you can't find Cornish game hens, you can use poussin, and if you are not sure about butterflying the birds, ask you butcher to do it for you. Serve these hot off the grill with a cooling citrus-honey sauce and a large crispy green salad.

To butterfly the hens, lay them breast-side down on a worktop and, using sharp scissors, cut down each side of the backbone. Discard the backbone. Open the hens up like a book and place them skin-side up in a ceramic dish.

Place the chiles/chillies, paprika, garlic, lemon zest and juice, and olive oil in a blender. Process until smooth and season with salt and pepper. Pour over the hens and place in the fridge uncovered for 6–24 hours (leaving them uncovered gives a crispier chicken skin).

To make the citrus-honey dipping sauce, whisk together all the ingredients in a small bowl. Cover and refrigerate until ready to use.

Heat the grill/barbecue to medium–high. Brush the grate with oil.

Remove the hens from the fridge and bring to room temperature.

Place the hens skin-side down on the grill and cook for 8–10 minutes until golden brown. Turn the hens over and turn down the heat or move to a cooler part of the grill. Continue to cook for 20 minutes. Check for doneness by inserting a knife to see that the meat is no longer pink and the juices run clear.

Remove the cooked hens from the grill to a chopping block, tent with foil, and rest for 5 minutes. To serve, cut the hens up and serve with the chilled citrus-honey dipping sauce.

FISH &
SEAFOOD

CEDAR PLANK SALMON

WITH SAKE

1 lb./450 g center-cut salmon, skin on
½ cup/125 ml sake
¼ cup/60 ml olive oil, plus extra for drizzling
1 tablespoon wasabi powder
10 shishito peppers, thinly sliced
sea salt and cracked black pepper
lemon wedges, to serve

cedar plank, 7 x 15 inches/18 x 38 cm

SERVES 4

Wooden planks are a great way to cook fish on the grill as they stop the fish from sticking to the metal grate. I use cedar planks, but there are other varieties of wood that lightly flavor the fish. The wooden planks are soaked in cold water first to prevent them burning over the hot coals.

Soak the cedar plank in cold water for a minimum of 3 hours, up to a maximum of 24 hours.

Rinse the salmon under cold water and pat dry with paper towels. Place in a ceramic baking dish.

In a small bowl, whisk together the sake, olive oil, wasabi powder, and a pinch of sea salt. Pour over the salmon and marinate for 20 minutes.

Heat the grill/barbecue to medium-high. Place the wet plank on the grill and leave it there for 6-8 minutes until the wood is charred on one side.

Turn the plank over. Remove the salmon from the marinade and place on top of the charred side of the plank. Sprinkle with the sliced shishito peppers and some cracked black pepper. Close the lid of the grill and cook for 15-20 minutes until the salmon is cooked. Times may differ depending on the thickness of the fish, so check for doneness by inserting a sharp knife into the fish— the flesh should be opaque in the middle.

Serve on the plank with lemon wedges and an extra drizzle of olive oil.

VINE-LEAF GRILLED TROUT

4 whole trout, butterflied
16 brined vine leaves
2 cups/500 g cooked wild rice
1 cup/90 g grapes, roughly chopped, plus 2 bunches of grapes for grilling
small bunch of dill, chopped
¼ cup/60 ml olive oil, plus extra for drizzling
¼ cup/60 ml freshly squeezed lemon juice
sea salt and cracked black pepper
oil, for brushing the grate
lemon wedges, to serve

kitchen twine/string

SERVES 4

Ask your fishmonger to butterfly the fish for you, but if that is not an option you can easily do it yourself. Take a sharp knife and run it along the under-belly of the fish, opening up the cavity. You can also make the stuffing with a variety of vegetables and fruits.

Rinse the fish under cold water and pat dry with paper towels.

Place four vine leaves close together on a work surface and place one trout on top. Repeat with the rest of the fish and vine leaves.

In a bowl mix together the cooked rice, chopped grapes, dill, oil, and lemon juice, and season with salt and pepper. Stuff each trout with a quarter of the rice mixture.

Fold the vine leaves around the fish and tie tightly with kitchen twine/string. Drizzle with a little olive oil and season with salt and pepper.

Heat the grill/barbecue to medium-high. Brush the grate with oil.

Place the bunches of grapes on the grill and cook until the grapes have caramelized and are beginning to burst open. Place on a platter.

Grill the trout for 5 minutes, then use a large spatula to turn them over. Reduce the heat or move the fish to a cooler part of the grill. Cook for another 5-8 minutes until the flesh is white and firm.

Remove the fish from the grill and cut off the twine. Serve with lemon wedges and the caramelized grapes.

GRILLED VINE LEAF WRAPPED SARDINES

12 sardines, gutted and cleaned
12 brined vine leaves
1 quantity Black Olive Stuffing
   (see below)
2 lemons, cut into thick slices
olive oil, for drizzling
sea salt and cracked black pepper

SERVES 4

This flavorsome recipe evokes memories of dining in Greek tavernas dotted along the beaches—long lazy lunches, eaten with your toes in the sand under canopies protecting you from the midday sun, and sipping icy cold retsina.

With a sharp knife, cut along the bottom of the sardines where they have been gutted. Rinse under cold water and pat them dry with paper towels.

Lay the vine leaves down on a work surface with the stem facing upward. Place a sardine on each leaf, then stuff each of the sardines with the Black Olive Stuffing. Fold the stem end of the leaf over the fish and tuck in both sides, then roll up.

Preheat the grill/barbecue to medium-high.

Grill the sardines for 5 minutes, then turn them over and grill for a further 5 minutes until cooked. Lay the lemon slices on the grill/barbecue and cook until charred.

Plate the sardines and grilled lemons, drizzle with olive oil, season with salt and pepper, and serve.

BLACK OLIVE STUFFING

1 cup/80 g toasted breadcrumbs
generous ½ cup/60 g pitted/stoned
   black olives, chopped
small bunch of flat-leaf parsley,
   roughly chopped
small bunch of oregano
½ cup/120 ml olive oil
sea salt and cracked black pepper

SERVES 4

This is a simple and fast stuffing, which can be put together in moments. The saltiness of the cured black olives and the aromatics of the herbs give it a wonderful Mediterranean feel. It can be used for all fish and meats. Change it up, if you like, by using different kinds of olives, such as Kalamata or Niçoise.

Put the breadcrumbs, olives, parsley, and oregano in a bowl. Pour in the olive oil, a little at a time (you may not need it all), and stir until the stuffing begins to bind together. Season with salt and pepper.

Store the stuffing in an airtight container in the fridge for up to 2 days.

BRANZINI IN A SALT CRUST

2 whole branzini
4 lemons, thinly sliced
12 lemon leaves (optional)
2 tablespoons freshly chopped
    rosemary
½ cup/120 ml white wine
cracked black pepper
8 cups/2 kg coarse sea salt

SERVES 4

Deliciously rich in flavor, branzini (also known as European sea bass) are the perfect fish to cook in a salt crust. You can cook any kind of fish in a salt crust and stuff with a variety of herbs and spices—here I have used a stuffing of lemons and lemon leaves, which adds a bright, sunny flavor. Serve with a robust green salad and chilled wine..

Heat the grill/barbecue to medium-high.

Rinse the fish under cold running water. Lay the fish on a work surface and pat dry with paper towels. Divide the lemon slices and leaves, if using, into four and stuff the cavity of each fish with them. Sprinkle with the rosemary and drizzle with the white wine. Season with cracked black pepper.

Pour the salt into a large bowl and add enough cold water to make it the consistency of wet sand, about 2½ cups/625 ml.

Spread half the salt mixture on a baking sheet and lay the fish on top. Cover the fish with the remainder of the salt and pack it tightly, making sure there are no holes for the steam to escape.

Place the baking sheet on top of the grill and close the lid. Bake for 40 minutes, then remove the fish from the grill and rest untouched for 5 minutes.

Using the back of large knife, crack open the salt crust. Remove the salt from around the fish and serve.

PAELLA ON THE GRILL

4 tablespoons/60 ml extra virgin
    olive oil
1 dry-cured Spanish chorizo sausage
    (about 8 oz./225 g), sliced
4 shallots, finely chopped
2 garlic cloves, finely chopped
1½ teaspoons Spanish smoked paprika
2 teaspoons hot red pepper flakes/
    chilli flakes
6 ripe tomatoes, roughly chopped
1½ cups/375 ml fish stock
1 cup/240 ml white wine
½ teaspoon saffron, soaked in
    3 tablespoons warm water
1½ cups/330 g paella rice
20 large shrimp/prawns, shells intact
20 mussels
sea salt and cracked black pepper
bunch of flat-leaf parsley, chopped,
    to garnish
lemon wedges, to serve

SERVES 6-8

Paella is a lovely dish to cook over an open fire. Gorgeous dark red tomatoes along with perfumed saffron, mixed with rice and topped with prawns all bubble together. Use good rice, such as Bomba, or any rice from Valencia in Spain. Serve with a fine Rioja.

Heat the grill/barbecue to medium-high.

Place a paella pan or large skillet/frying pan on the grill and add 2 tablespoons of the olive oil. Add the chorizo to the pan and cook for about 2–3 minutes until the sausage is brown and crispy. Remove from the pan to a plate and set aside.

Add the remaining olive oil, the shallots, and garlic and cook for 2 minutes until golden, then add the paprika and hot red pepper flakes/chilli flakes and stir to combine. Tip in the tomatoes and, stirring occasionally, cook for about 5 minutes until they have broken down into a sauce. Season with salt and pepper.

Pour the stock, wine, and saffron into a pan and place on the grill. Bring to the boil, then move to a cooler part of the grill to keep at a simmer.

Stir the rice into the tomato mixture and cook for 2 minutes. Pour the stock mixture over the rice and stir. Bring to the boil, then move to a cooler part of the grill and simmer for 8–10 minutes without stirring.

Add the shrimp/prawns, mussels, and chorizo and gently push down into the rice. Cover the pan with foil and cook for another 10–15 minutes until the shrimp are cooked through and the mussels have opened up (discard any that have not opened).

Remove the pan from the grill and rest for 5 minutes, then remove the foil. Sprinkle with the parsley and serve with lemon wedges.

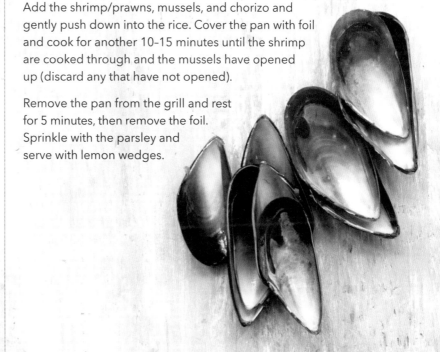

CLAM STEAMERS

WITH CALABRIAN CHILES

¼ cup/60 ml olive oil
2 garlic cloves, finely minced
1 large yellow onion, diced
1 dry-cured chorizo sausage (about
   8 oz./225 g), sliced
12 ripe cherry tomatoes
1 bay leaf
½ teaspoon Spanish smoked paprika
2 Calabrian chiles/chillies,
   roughly chopped
3 cups/700 ml dry white wine
30 Little Neck clams, cleaned
sea salt and cracked black pepper
crusty loaf or baguette, to serve

SERVES 4

Serve this with plenty of crusty bread to soak up the wonderful smoky sauce the clams are nestled in. This is a real summer dish for the barbecue, and you can use any kind of clams or mussels and swap out white wine for Madeira wine or beer. The Calabrian chiles bring a pleasantly warm heat to the dish.

Heat the grill/barbecue to medium-high.

Place a large cast-iron pan on the grill and pour in the olive oil. Add the garlic and onion and cook for 2–3 minutes. Add the chorizo and continue to cook for another 5 minutes, stirring frequently.

Stir in the tomatoes, bay leaf, paprika, and chiles/chillies and cook for a further 3 minutes.

Pour in the wine and season with salt and pepper. Bring to the boil and cook for 6–8 minutes until the sauce thickens and the tomatoes are broken down.

Add the clams to the pan. Cover and cook for 6–8 minutes, stirring halfway through, until all the clams have opened. Discard any that stay closed.

Serve in bowls, with bread on the side for mopping up all the juices.

GARLIC CHILI SHRIMP

2 lb./900 g shrimp/prawns, heads on
1 whole head of garlic, cloves separated
    and peeled
1 tablespoon hot red pepper flakes/
    chilli flakes
¼ cup/60 ml olive oil
2 tablespoons oregano leaves
sea salt and cracked black pepper
good crusty bread, to serve

SERVES 4-6

Set a large cast-iron pan in the middle of the table with juicy garlic chili prawns to be eaten with your hands and the juices mopped up with crusty bread. You can use any type of shrimp/prawn that has the head and shell intact, simply increase the cooking time slightly for larger ones.

Place the shrimp/prawns in a large bowl and set aside.

Put the garlic cloves in a food processor along with the hot red pepper flakes/chilli flakes and oil. Process to break garlic into small chunks.

Pour the mixture over the shrimp/prawns, sprinkle with the oregano, and season with salt and pepper. Toss to combine. Set aside for 5 minutes while you heat the grill/barbecue to medium-high.

Place a large cast-iron pan on the grill and heat until just smoking. Place the shrimp/prawns and all the juices in the hot pan and cook for 6-8 minutes, turning every few minutes, until they are cooked through. Serve alongside a basket of crusty bread.

GRILLED LOBSTERS
WITH FLAVORED BUTTERS

4 cooked lobsters, about 2 lb./
    900 g each, steamed or boiled
sea salt and cracked black pepper
oil, for brushing
good crusty bread, to serve

NORI SEAWEED BUTTER
2 sheets nori seaweed, crumbled
2 sticks/225 g salted butter

WASABI BUTTER
2 tablespoons wasabi powder
2 sticks/225 g salted butter

GARLIC & CHILI BUTTER
6 garlic cloves, peeled
1 jalapeño chile/chilli, roughly chopped
2 sticks/225 g salted butter

SERVES 4-6

Lobsters are so easy to throw on the grill and serve up with an array of flavored butters. Steam or boil the lobsters first and then put them on the grill, as this makes the meat juicy and tender.

To make the seaweed butter, place the nori and butter in the bowl of a food processor and pulse until smooth. Season with salt and pepper and spoon into a small bowl. Clean the food processor bowl.

For the wasabi butter, add the wasabi and butter to the food processor and pulse to combine, then season with salt and pepper and spoon into a small bowl. Clean the food processor bowl.

Lastly, for the garlic and chilli butter, place the garlic, jalapeño, and butter in the food processor. Pulse to combine completely, season with salt and pepper, and spoon into a small bowl.

Heat the grill/barbecue to medium-high. Brush the grate with oil.

Crack the claws and brush the lobsters with olive oil, then season with salt and pepper. Using sharp scissors, cut the underneath of the lobster from top to bottom. Place the lobsters on the grill and cook for 5 minutes, then use tongs to turn them over and continue to cook for another 5 minutes, or until the flesh is white and has no translucency.

Serve the lobsters along with the flavored butters and crusty bread.

COCONUT & LIME SHRIMP SKEWERS

2 lb./900 g peeled shrimp/prawns,
 tails on
14-fl oz/400-ml can of unsweetened
 coconut milk
1 tablespoon curry powder
1 tablespoon ground turmeric
1 tablespoon finely minced
 fresh ginger
1 teaspoon hot red pepper flakes/
 chilli flakes
3 tablespoons fish sauce
½ cup/35 g dried coconut flakes
16 makrut lime leaves
lime wedges, to serve

Himalayan pink salt block
8 wooden skewers, soaked
 in cold water

SERVES 4

Himalayan salt blocks are so pretty to look at, with shades of pink marbled through the salt, and are perfect to use as a serving dish for sushi or chilled fruits in summer. You can also cook meat, vegetables, and fish on them as they work really well on a grill. Afterward, simply rinse off under cold water, let dry, and they are ready to use again.

Rinse the shrimp/prawns under cold running water and pat dry with paper towels. Place in a ceramic baking dish.

In a medium-sized bowl, whisk together the coconut milk, curry powder, turmeric, ginger, hot red pepper flakes/chilli flakes, and fish sauce. Pour the marinade over the shrimp and add the coconut flakes. Toss to make sure they are completely covered. Cover and refrigerate until ready to use.

Place the salt block on a cold grill/barbecue and heat to 400°F (200°C). Once it has reached this temperature, let the salt block continue to heat for another 30 minutes.

While the block is heating, prepare the skewers. Remove the shrimp from the refrigerator and divide into eight portions. Thread onto the wooden skewers, alternating with the lime leaves. Brush the shrimp with a little more of the marinade, then discard any remaining marinade.

Place the skewers on the salt block and cook for 4 minutes, then turn them over and continue to cook for another 4 minutes until the centers of the shrimp are opaque.

Serve with lime wedges for squeezing over.

POKE BOWLS

1 lb./450 g very fresh sushi-grade
  ahi tuna
vegetable oil, if you wish to grill
  the fish
2 tablespoons toasted sesame oil
2 tablespoons tamari or soy sauce
grated zest and freshly squeezed juice
  of 1 lime, plus wedges for serving
1 tablespoon mirin
1 jalapeño chile/chilli, finely diced
1 tablespoon finely chopped
  pickled ginger
sea salt and cracked black pepper
2 cups/500 g cooked sushi rice
  or white rice
6 scallions/spring onions, thinly sliced
6 radishes, thinly sliced
1 avocado, peeled, pitted/stoned,
  and sliced into wedges
1 Persian cucumber, thinly sliced
sesame seeds, for sprinkling
Nori Komi Furikake
  (Asian seaweed mix)

SERVES 2

Originating in Hawaii where sea fish is at its best, the poké bowl is made with yellowtail or ahi tuna and is served as an appetizer. Now that the poké bowl has traveled outside of the islands, it has taken on a new life. It is popping up with an assortment of vegetables, noodles, pickles, tofu, and all things healthy and fresh. If you are not crazy about raw fish, then grill it for a couple of minutes on each side.

Rinse the tuna under cold running water and pat dry with paper towels. Cut the tuna into 1-inch/2.5-cm chunks and place in a bowl. (If you prefer the tuna lightly cooked, grill it for just a few minutes on each side until slightly charred but still pink in the middle, and then cut into chunks.)

In another bowl whisk together the sesame oil, tamari, lime zest and juice, mirin, jalapeño, and ginger. Season to taste, pour over the tuna, and toss to combine.

Divide the rice between two serving bowls and top with the tuna, scallions/spring onions, radishes, avocado, and cucumber. Drizzle with some of the dressing and sprinkle with sesame seeds and Nori Komi Furikake.

Serve with lime wedges for squeezing over.

SALADS &
VEGETABLE SIDES

PICKLED GREEN TOMATO PANZANELLA

¼ cup/60 ml white wine vinegar
1 teaspoon thinly sliced chives
¼ cup/60 ml extra virgin olive oil,
   plus extra to serve
1 garlic clove, finely minced
1½ cups/250 g heirloom/heritage
   cherry tomatoes, halved
1 cup/100 g Pickled Green Tomatoes
   (see page 170)
1 cup/15 g basil leaves, roughly torn
1 small red onion, thinly sliced
1 tablespoon capers
sea salt and cracked black pepper

CROUTONS
6 thick slices ciabatta bread
olive oil, for brushing
2 garlic cloves

SERVES 4-6

Panzanella is the perfect answer for using up day-old bread. It just gets better as it sits and soaks up all the vinegars and pickled brine. Make it for supper or outdoor lunches—it is great as a picnic food as it transports so easily in containers. This recipe requires the Pickled Green Tomatoes on page 170 so you'll need to get ahead with those before you can begin to prepare this.

Preheat a broiler/grill pan over medium-high heat.

Begin by preparing the croutons. Brush the sliced bread with olive oil and cook on the hot pan until golden and slightly charred. When toasted, set aside to cool, then rub with the garlic cloves. Roughly chop the toast into 1-inch/2.5-cm croutons.

Put the vinegar, chives, and olive oil in a large bowl and whisk together. Add the minced garlic and season with salt and pepper. Add the croutons, heirloom/heritage cherry tomatoes, Pickled Green Tomatoes, basil, onion, and capers, and mix together. Cover and set aside for at least 1 hour before serving.

Spoon the panzanella onto a serving dish. Drizzle with a little extra olive oil, sprinkle with salt and pepper, and serve immediately.

GRILLED TOMATO CAPRESE

2 lb./900 g cherry tomatoes
  (about 6 branches)
sea salt and cracked black pepper
oil, for brushing the grate
basil leaves, to garnish

RICOTTA
8 cups/1.9 litres whole milk
1 cup/250 ml heavy/double cream
⅓ cup/80 ml organic white
  distilled vinegar or freshly
  squeezed lemon juice

PESTO
2 cups/100 g basil leaves
½ cup/35 g freshly grated
  Parmesan cheese
½ cup/55 g chopped almonds
2 garlic cloves, minced
½ cup/125 ml extra virgin olive oil
1 tablespoon freshly squeezed
  lemon juice

SERVES 6–8

Making your own ricotta is a breeze and absolutely delicious. The same goes for pesto—try this and you won't buy ready-made again. This salad is perfect for a summer lunch, served with grilled breads and chilled rosé.

To make the ricotta, pour the milk and cream into a large pan and place over medium heat. Place a candy thermometer on the side of the pan and heat to 190°F (88°C).

Remove the pan from the heat and add the vinegar or lemon juice. Using a wooden spoon, stir the mixture very slowly a few times, then cover with a kitchen towel and set aside for 1 hour.

Line a strainer/sieve with cheesecloth/muslin and place over a bowl large enough to catch the whey. Gently pour the ricotta curds into the cheesecloth and leave to drain for 45 minutes. Place the ricotta in a glass storage container and season with salt and pepper, then cover and refrigerate.

To make the pesto, place the basil, cheese, almonds, and garlic in the bowl of a food processor and pulse a couple of times. With the motor running, pour in the olive oil in a steady stream. Add the lemon juice and season with salt and pepper. Pulse a few times to combine, then pour into a glass storage container.

Heat the grill/barbecue to medium–high. Brush the grate with oil.

Place the tomatoes on the grill and cook for about 4 minutes until they are bursting open and charred.

To serve, spoon the ricotta onto a platter and top with the grilled tomatoes, then drizzle with the pesto and garnish with the basil. Store the remaining pesto in the fridge for another use. It will keep for up to a week.

GRILLED HEIRLOOM GAZPACHO CUPS

12 ripe but firm heirloom tomatoes
2 garlic cloves, unpeeled
1 yellow onion, cut in half, unpeeled
1 red (bell) pepper
2 Serrano chiles/chillies, red or green
2 Persian cucumbers, roughly chopped
¼ cup/60 ml extra virgin olive oil,
    plus extra for drizzling
¼ cup/60 ml Jerez sherry vinegar
sea salt and cracked black pepper
oil, for brushing the grate
tomato flowers or herbs, to garnish
    (optional)

SERVES 6-8

Grilling the tomatoes, peppers, chiles, and garlic gives a wonderfully deep smoky and sweet flavor to this gazpacho. Serving it in cups makes a fun way to start a party. Use good Spanish sherry vinegar from Jerez de La Frontera to flavor.

Heat the grill/barbecue to medium-high. Brush the grate with oil.

Place the tomatoes, garlic, onion, pepper, and chiles/chillies on the grill and cook, turning often, until charred and softened but still keeping their shape.

Remove the vegetables from the grill and place on a cutting board. Peel the onion and garlic and cut off the ends.

Place all the grilled vegetables and the cucumbers in a blender along with the olive oil and vinegar and process until you have a slightly chunky soup. Season with salt and pepper and chill in the fridge for 2-24 hours.

Fill cups with the chilled gazpacho, drizzle with a little olive oil, and garnish with tomato flowers or herbs, if using.

LOBSTER & TARRAGON POTATO SALAD

2 cooked lobsters (about 2 lb./
  900 g each)
1½ lb./680 g baby potatoes
1 head frisée or endive/chicory
2 tablespoons tarragon vinegar
2 tablespoons mayonnaise
1 tablespoon wholegrain mustard
¼ cup/60 ml extra virgin olive oil
1 cup/20 g tarragon leaves
sea salt and cracked black pepper

SERVES 4

Is there anything better in the world than freshly cooked lobster and a glass of very cold white wine? This is a delicate salad perfumed with tarragon, perfectly matched for summer eating.

Crack the shell of the lobsters and pull out all the meat. Place in a large bowl and break the meat in to large chunks.

Steam the potatoes over a large pot of boiling water for about 10-15 minutes, or until a sharp knife easily pierces through them. Rinse the frisée or endive/chicory in cold water and dry it. Tear the leaves and set aside.

In a large serving bowl whisk together the vinegar, mayonnaise, and mustard. Pour in the olive oil and whisk to combine. Season with salt and pepper.

Add the lobster, warm potatoes, frisée or endive, and tarragon leaves. Toss together, sprinkle with cracked black pepper, and serve.

COOKS' NOTE: Reserve the lobster heads and shells to make fish stock.

CHARRED TREVISO SALAD

½ cup/55 g almonds, roughly chopped
2-oz/56-g can of anchovies
2 cups/100 g panko breadcrumbs
3 tablespoons salted capers
¼ cup/60 ml olive oil
4 small Treviso chicory/radicchio,
    cut in half lengthwise
¼ cup/30g grated Parmesan cheese
    (optional)
cracked black pepper
oil, for brushing the grate

SERVES 6-8

Charred Treviso bathed in an anchovy and almond dressing is a delicious accompaniment to any barbecue. It's a hardy but milder relative of radicchio and has pretty, long leaves that are tinged with green and white. The anchovy and breadcrumbs add sweetness to this salad.

Place the almonds and anchovies (there's no need to drain them) in a food processor and pulse to a rough consistency. Pour the mixture into a bowl and add the breadcrumbs, capers, and half the olive oil. Toss together and season with pepper.

Heat a pan over medium-high heat, add the breadcrumb mixture, and toast until golden brown. Set aside.

Heat the grill/barbecue to medium-high. Brush the grate with oil.

Place the Treviso on a baking sheet and brush with the remaining olive oil. Grill for 2-3 minutes on each side until slightly charred and wilted.

Remove them to a platter and scatter with the breadcrumb mix. Sprinkle with the Parmesan, if using, and season with a little more black pepper.

OUZO WATERMELON SALAD

1 watermelon
½ cup/120 ml ouzo
4 Persian cucumbers
1 lb./450 g feta cheese, crumbled
1¼ cup/130 g pitted/stoned
    Kalamata olives
¼ cup/60 ml extra virgin olive oil
small bunch of oregano
sea salt and cracked black pepper

SERVES 6

Serve this refreshingly simple, eye-catching, grown-up salad when the mercury starts to rise. The ouzo infuses the watermelon just a little, enhancing all that sweet goodness. It's the perfect salad to pack up and take to the beach to enjoy while watching the sun set.

Place the watermelon on a work surface and cut into quarters. Remove the skin, cut the flesh into 1½-inch/4-cm cubes, and place in a large bowl.

Pour the ouzo over the watermelon and gently toss together to make sure all the pieces are coated. Marinate for 20 minutes.

Chop the cucumber into 1½-inch/4-cm chunks and add to the watermelon. Add the feta and olives and pour over the olive oil. Season with salt and pepper and gently toss to combine.

Arrange on a large platter and scatter over the oregano.

JICAMA, APPLE, & FENNEL SLAW

1 small jicama
4 red beets/beetroots
4 golden beets/beetroots
1 fennel bulb
1 Poblano chile/chilli
¼ cup/60 ml bottled yuzu juice
2 tablespoons ponzu sauce
3 tablespoons mirin
2 tablespoons maple syrup
grated zest and freshly squeezed
    juice of 1 lime
small bunch of marjoram

SERVES 6

Jicama is a wonderful bulbous vegetable commonly found in Mexican cooking. It has a crisp texture, similar to an apple, and is eaten raw in summer and winter slaws or as a crudité. Yuzu is a sour Japanese citrus fruit, which is a bit like a cross between an orange and lime. It can be a little hard to find fresh, but you can source bottled yuzu on the internet or from Asian stores. It is a useful pantry staple, to be used in dressings, drizzled over ceviche, or splashed into a weekend cocktail. You can substitute it with grapefruit or lime juice.

Peel the jicama and beets/beetroot and set aside.

Using a mandoline, one by one, shred the jicama, beets, fennel, and Poblano chile/chilli and place in a large bowl.

Whisk together the yuzu, ponzu, mirin, maple syrup, and lime zest and juice. Pour over the slaw and toss to combine. Cover and refrigerate for about 30 minutes to allow the flavors to meld together.

Tip out onto a large platter, sprinkle with the marjoram, and serve while still chilled.

SALAD NIÇOISE

6 eggs
leaves of 1 head butter/round lettuce,
   rinsed
8 oz./225 g best-quality preserved tuna
   in oil
1 red onion, thinly sliced
1 cup/150g Haricots Verts with Pickled
   Onions (see page 166)
18 anchovy fillets
2/3 cup/65 g Niçoise olives
2 cups/340 g cherry tomatoes, halved
1/4 cup/60 ml tarragon vinegar
1/2 cup/125 ml extra virgin olive oil
sea salt and cracked black pepper

SERVES 4

This is by no means a traditional Niçoise. Enjoy the pickle flavors alongside the tuna and crispy lettuce, grill up some thick crusty bread and dig in. Use the best tuna you can find.

Cook the eggs in boiling water for 4 minutes, then cool under cold running water and peel. Set aside.

To prepare the salad, tear the lettuce leaves and arrange them in a large shallow bowl. Add the tuna, onion, Haricots Verts with Pickled Onions, anchovies, olives, and tomatoes.

Cut the eggs into quarters and arrange them on top of the salad.

Whisk together the vinegar and oil and season with salt and pepper.

Drizzle a little vinaigrette over the salad, gently toss, and serve immediately.

COOKS' NOTE: Reserve any extra vinaigrette for another use.

GRILLED SUMMER ZUCCHINI
WITH BASIL SALT

¼ cup/65 g coarse sea salt
12 large basil leaves
16 green and golden zucchini/
    courgettes
½ cup/120 ml avocado oil
¼ cup/60 ml Champagne vinegar
10 zucchini/courgette flowers,
    stamens removed
cracked black pepper
oil, for brushing the grate

SERVES 6

Bright yellow squash blossoms are beautiful and delicious at the same time. They shout out summer in all its glory, just as daffodils announce springtime. Grilling the zucchini/courgettes and their flowers on hot coals, then sprinkling with basil salt, is simple and perfect for any occasion.

Preheat the oven to 250°F (120°C) Gas ½.

Pulse the salt and basil in a food processor, then spread the mixture out on a baking sheet. Bake in the preheated oven for 30 minutes until dry. Pour into a sterilized glass jar with a tight-fitting lid and set aside. (Any unused basil salt will keep for 2 weeks stored this way.)

Slice the zucchini/courgettes in half lengthwise (or quarter them if they are large) and arrange on a baking sheet. Whisk together the oil and vinegar and season with salt and pepper. Pour this over the zucchini and toss to make sure they are well covered.

Heat the grill/barbecue to medium-high. Brush the grate with oil.

Grill the zucchini for 3-4 minutes on each side until they are slightly charred and golden brown, then plate. Place the zucchini flowers on the grill and cook for about a minute on each side, then add to the zucchini.

Sprinkle with the basil salt and cracked black pepper and serve

GRILLED AVOCADOS
WITH MESCAL & LIME DRESSING

¼ cup/60 ml orange blossom honey
¼ cup/60 ml extra virgin olive oil
¼ cup/60ml Mescal
grated zest and freshly squeezed juice
    of 2 large limes
4 avocados, halved, and pitted/stoned
sea salt and cracked black pepper
oil, for brushing the grate

SERVES 6

Avocados trees grow all over California and their fruits are a big part of everyday meals. Grilling them deepens the flavor, while dousing them in a perfumed Mescal and lime dressing is divine. Next time you make guacamole, try charring the avocados on the grill before mashing them.

In a small bowl whisk together the honey, oil, Mescal, and lime zest and juice. Season with salt and pepper and set aside.

Heat the grill/barbecue to medium-high. Brush the grate with oil.

Place the avocados cut-side down on the grill and cook for about 3-4 minutes until slightly charred and browned. Turn them over and cook for another 2 minutes.

Remove from the grill and place on a platter, drizzle with the Mescal and lime dressing, and serve.

MEXICAN GRILLED CORN

1 cup/250 g Mexican crema or
  crème fraîche
½ cup/125 g mayonnaise
1 jalapeño chile/chilli, seeded and
  finely diced
1 tablespoon chili/chilli powder,
  plus extra to garnish
1½ cups/160 g Cotija cheese (or feta
  cheese, if you cannot find Cojita)
6 corn cobs in the husk
3 tablespoons olive oil
small bunch of cilantro/coriander,
  finely chopped
sea salt
oil, for brushing the grate
lime wedges, to serve

SERVES 6

Grilled corn slathered in cream, cheese, and chiles, and finished off with freshly squeezed limes are known as 'elotes' in Mexico and sold as street food. Use the husk as a handle when eating.

Heat the grill/barbecue to medium-high. Brush the grate with oil.

Place the crema, mayonnaise, jalapeño, chili/chilli powder, and half the cheese in a medium-sized bowl and mix together. Season with salt.

Peel the corn husks back and twist to make a handle. Brush the corn with the olive oil and place on the grill. Cook for about 10–12 minutes, turning every 3-4 minutes, until the corn is golden and caramelized.

When the corn is ready, generously brush the crema mixture over the kernels. Sprinkle over the remaining cheese and the chopped cilantro/coriander and finish with a dusting of chili powder.

Serve with lime wedges for squeezing.

ROASTED STUFFED TOMATOES

6 large heirloom tomatoes
1 cup/100 g pitted/stoned Kalamata
  olives, roughly chopped
1 cup/135 g feta cheese, crumbled
2 tablespoons oregano leaves
½ cup/115 g pesto (store-bought
  or see page 80)
sea salt and cracked black pepper
olive oil, for drizzling

SERVES 6

Roasted tomatoes are one of the highlights of summer cooking, especially if you choose heirloom varieties for their kaleidoscope of colors and rich taste. After cooking on the grill, drizzle the tomatoes with aromatic pesto for a melt-in-your-mouth delight.

Heat the grill/barbecue to medium-high.

Using a serrated knife, slice the tops off the tomatoes and set aside.

Using a teaspoon, scoop out the insides of the tomatoes and place the pulp in a medium-sized bowl. Add the olives, feta, and oregano and stir to combine. Season with salt and pepper—you will only need a touch of salt as the feta is a salty cheese.

Place the tomatoes in a snug-fitting baking dish. Stuff each tomato with the feta mixture and place the tomato tops back on. Drizzle with olive oil.

Place the baking dish on the grate of the barbecue and close the lid. Cook for 10 minutes, then check them. You may need to either reduce the heat or move them to a cooler part of the grill. Continue to cook until the tomatoes are soft but are still keeping their shape.

When ready, remove the tomatoes from the grill, drizzle with a little pesto, and serve.

ROASTED CAULIFLOWER & RED WALNUT ROMESCO

1 head of cauliflower
¼ cup/60 ml white wine
1 tablespoon salted capers
2 tablespoons oregano leaves
cracked black pepper
extra virgin olive oil, for drizzling
sumac, for sprinkling

ROMESCO SAUCE
1 cup/125 g red walnuts,
    or regular walnuts
2 cups/300 g heirloom cherry tomatoes
4 large garlic cloves, smashed
1 red (bell) pepper, quartered
¼ cup/60 ml olive oil, plus
    2 tablespoons
2 teaspoons harissa (store-bought
    or see page 47)
1 tablespoon freshly squeezed
    lemon juice
sea salt and cracked black pepper

SERVES 4-6

Red walnuts are so pretty—when you crack open the shells a dark red walnut falls out. You can substitute regular walnuts if you can't source the red ones. Make the sauce ahead of time, then all you have to do is roast the cauliflower. You can also cut the cauliflower into thick slices and brush with olive oil before grilling.

Preheat the oven to 425°F (220°C) Gas 7.

To make the sauce, place the walnuts in a small cast-iron pan and roast over medium heat for 5 minutes, then set aside.

Toss the tomatoes, garlic, and (bell) pepper with the ¼ cup/60 ml olive oil, then tip onto a baking sheet and season with black pepper. Roast in the preheated oven for 20-25 minutes until charred. Remove from the oven and cool for 5 minutes.

Place the roasted vegetables in a food processor along with the remaining 2 tablespoons of oil, the harissa, and lemon juice and pulse until you have a thick, slightly chunky sauce. Season with salt and pepper and set aside. This can be made one day ahead and stored in the fridge.

Place the cauliflower in a Dutch oven/casserole dish, pour in the wine, then sprinkle with the capers and oregano leaves. Drizzle with olive oil, season with cracked black pepper, and place the lid on. Roast in the oven (also at 425°F (220°C) Gas 7) for 40 minutes, then remove the lid and continue to cook for another 15 minutes until cooked. You can check the doneness by inserting a sharp knife into the cauliflower.

Sprinkled with sumac and serve with the Romesco sauce on the side.

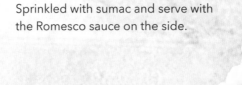

SAVORY TARTS
& FLATBREADS

HEIRLOOM TOMATO & BLACK GARLIC GALETTE

10 mixed heirloom tomatoes
10 heirloom cherry tomatoes
1 lb./450 g ready-rolled puff pastry
3 tablespoons chopped black garlic
a few thyme sprigs
1 egg, beaten
coarse sea salt
extra virgin olive oil, for drizzling

a baking sheet lined with baking parchment

SERVES 6-8

In August, when the farmers' market is at its best, you will see stands decked with bejeweled tomatoes of every type and size. From big, fat, rosy red tomatoes to dark-purple and bright-green striped ones, they all make a huge statement. Have fun with this galette and mix and match colors and varieties.

Preheat the oven to 425°F (220°C) Gas 7.

Cut the tomatoes into thick slices and the cherry tomatoes in half (or leave these whole if you wish).

Place the pastry on the prepared baking sheet. Using a knife, score a ¼-inch/5-mm border on each side of the pastry (but take care not to cut all the way through the pastry).

Top the pastry with the tomatoes, leaving the border clear. Sprinkle the garlic over the tomatoes and top with the thyme sprigs.

Brush the edges of the pastry with the beaten egg, then bake in the preheated oven for 20 minutes until brown and crusty.

Remove from the oven, sprinkle with salt, and drizzle with olive oil.

PICKLED STRAWBERRY & GRAPE BURRATA TARTINES

loaf of rustic bread, sliced
olive oil
1 lb./450 g burrata
sea salt and cracked black pepper
flowering herbs, to garnish (optional)

PICKLED STRAWBERRIES
24 strawberries, plus some leaves
   (optional)
1 cup/250 ml white balsamic vinegar
2 tablespoons kosher salt
2 tablespoons white sugar
1 tablespoon pink peppercorns

PICKLED GRAPES
2 cups/300 g red grapes
1 cup/250 ml apple cider vinegar
1 tablespoon turbinado
   (or light brown) sugar
1 teaspoon kosher salt
1 red chile/chilli

SERVES 6-8

When you visit a farmers' market it is always worth over-buying, especially in summer when the stalls are weighed down with plump, juicy fruits and berries. You can either roast the excess or pickle it. Serve the burrata torn open with the fruit pickles and grilled bread on a big wooden board along with chilled wines. Dinner in itself.

To make the pickled strawberries, pack them, and the leaves if using, in a sterilized jar with a tight-fitting lid. Place the vinegar, salt, sugar, and peppercorns in a pan with ¼ cup/60 ml water and bring to the boil over medium–high heat. Cook for 3 minutes, then pour over the strawberries. Set aside to cool, then place the lid on tightly and refrigerate overnight.

To make the pickled grapes, pack the grapes into a sterilized jar with a tight-fitting lid. Place the vinegar, sugar, and salt in a pan with ¼ cup/60 ml water and bring to the boil over a medium high heat. Cook for 3 minutes, then pour over the grapes and add the red chile/chilli. Set aside to cool, then place the lid on tightly and refrigerate overnight.

Heat the grill/barbecue to medium–high.

Brush the sliced bread on both sides liberally with olive oil. Place on the grill and toast each side for about 2 minutes until golden brown and slightly charred.

Spread each piece of bread with burrata and top with the pickled strawberries and grapes. Season with salt and pepper, and garnish with fresh flowering herbs, if using.

CARAMELIZED BEET TATIN

13 oz./375 g ready-rolled puff pastry
1 tablespoon butter
1 tablespoon maple syrup
handful of thyme sprigs
4 red beets/beetroots, peeled and
    thinly sliced
Marinated Goat Cheese (see below)
sea salt
all-purpose/plain flour, for dusting

a 10-inch/25-cm cast-iron pan

SERVES 4-6

Don't think a tatin is only for apples and stone fruits. Here is a delicious, healthy, and savory turn of events using fresh beets as the star. Pair with an earthy, fresh herb like thyme and top it off with delicious marinated goat cheese dripping in olive oil and lemons. It's just the right size for a lunch party.

Preheat the oven to 425°F (220°C) Gas 7.

On a lightly floured work surface, dust the puff pastry with flour and cut out a circle 11 inch/28 cm in diameter.

Set the cast-iron pan over medium–high heat, and melt the butter and maple syrup. Stir until combined and cook for about 5 minutes, until bubbling and caramelized.

Remove the pan from the heat and scatter 6 sprigs of thyme into the butter-syrup mixture. Arrange the beet/beetroot slices in a layer of concentric circles covering the base of the pan, then return the pan to the heat and continue to cook for a further 5 minutes.

Lay the pastry on top of the beets, tucking in the overhanging edges, then transfer the pan to the preheated oven. Bake for 15 minutes until golden brown. Remove from the oven and leave to cool slightly. Carefully invert the tatin onto a serving plate.

Top with crumbled Marinated Goat Cheese and some of the remaining thyme sprigs. Sprinkle with a little sea salt to finish.

MARINATED GOAT CHEESE

8 oz./225 g goat cheese
1 lemon
4 bay leaves
½ teaspoon black peppercorns
½ teaspoon dried chili flakes
1 cup/240 ml extra virgin olive oil

*a 1-quart/1-litre glass jar, sterilized
(see page 4)*

YIELDS 1 QUART/LITRE

Marinated goat cheese will last for a couple of months in the fridge. As well as using it in the Caramelized Beet Tatin (above), it's also lovely on a cheese board, pizza or pasta.

Roll the goat cheese into small balls.

Peel the lemon and cut the skin into strips. (You don't need the lemon flesh or juice, so reserve this for another use.)

Layer the goat cheese, lemon peel, bay leaves, peppercorns, and hot red pepper flakes/chilli flakes in the sterilized glass jar. Pour over the olive oil making sure to cover the goat cheese.

Store the cheese in the jar in the fridge for up to 2 months.

PISSALADIÈRE
WITH PROVENÇAL OLIVE RELISH

3 cups/375 g plain/all-purpose flour
¼ oz./7 g fast-action dried yeast
2 tablespoons thyme leaves, plus a few
    sprigs to garnish
½ teaspoon salt
1¼ cups/300 ml warm water
½ cup/120 ml olive oil, plus extra
    for drizzling
8 red onions, thinly sliced
Provençal Olive Relish (see page 165)
12–14 anchovy fillets
15 pitted/stoned black olives

a baking sheet, oiled

SERVES 4

Pissaladière can be cooked in a very hot oven or on the grill. The saltiness of the anchovies and sweetness of the caramelized onions with olive relish is sensational, however it is cooked. You'll need to prepare the Provençal Olive Relish on page 165 for this recipe.

Begin by making the dough. Place the flour, yeast, thyme, and salt in a ceramic bowl, and mix together. Stir in the water and ¼ cup/60 ml olive oil until combined. Cover with plastic wrap/clingfilm and set aside to rise for 2½–3 hours until it doubles in size.

To caramelize the onions, place a large skillet/frying pan over medium-low heat and add the remaining ¼ cup/60 ml olive oil and the onions. Cook for about 25 minutes, stirring occasionally, until the onions are golden brown and soft. Set aside.

Preheat the oven to 500°F (260°C) Gas 10, or as high as it will go.

Turn the risen dough out onto the oiled baking sheet. Gently press the dough with the palms of your hands, stretching it to the edges of the pan. Spread the onions over the dough and randomly dollop the Provençal Olive Relish on top. Arrange the anchovies and olives on top.

Bake in the preheated oven for about 15–20 minutes until the dough is golden and crispy.

Slice into portions and serve garnished with sprigs of thyme and a drizzle of olive oil.

COOKS' NOTE: You can also cook the pissaladière on a very hot grill/barbecue with a lid.

GRILLED PIZZA

WITH OYSTERS & PARMESAN CREAM

1¾ cups/220 g all-purpose/plain flour
1½ teaspoons fast-action dried yeast
1 teaspoon sea salt
⅔ cup/160 ml warm water
1 cup/100 g grated Parmesan cheese,
    plus extra for sprinkling
1 cup/250 ml heavy/double cream
16 medium or 8 large freshly
    shucked oysters
4 Calabrian chiles/chillies, sliced
a pinch of fennel pollen
a handful of arugula/rocket leaves
extra virgin olive oil, for oiling the bowl
all-purpose/plain flour, for dusting
oil, for brushing the grate

SERVES 2

Pizzas are so easy to cook on the grill, and fast too. You don't need a pizza stone or have to preheat the oven. Grilling transforms the dough into a wonderful charred crispy base for your favorite toppings. You can also use ready-made pizza dough, if you wish, to make your summer easier.

Oil a large bowl and set aside.

Place the flour, yeast, and salt in the bowl of a food processor. With the motor running, add the water to the flour mixture in a steady stream until all the liquid is incorporated and the dough forms a ball—this takes about 3 minutes.

Place the dough on a floured worktop and knead to form a ball. Place in the oiled bowl and cover with a kitchen towel. Set aside in a warm place for about 3 hours to double in size.

To make the Parmesan cream, place the cheese and cream in a saucepan and bring to the boil. Reduce to a simmer and, stirring continuously, cook until the cheese has melted and you have a sauce. Remove from the heat and set aside.

Heat the grill/barbecue to medium–high. Brush the grate with oil.

Remove the dough from the bowl and cut into two pieces. Roll each piece out into a circle about 10 inches/25 cm in diameter.

If your grill/barbecue is big enough, you can cook both pizzas at the same time; if not, cook one at time. Place the dough on the hot grill and cook for 3–5 minutes until golden and charred. Turn the crusts over and liberally spread with the Parmesan cream. Top with the oysters and chiles/chillies and sprinkle with some fennel pollen.

Close the lid and cook for another 5 minutes until the oysters are cooked through and the pizza is charred and crusty.

To serve, remove from the grill onto a wooden board, sprinkle with some grated Parmesan and top with arugula/rocket leaves.

PROSCIUTTO & FIG GRILLED FLATBREADS

1¾ cups/220 g all-purpose/plain flour
1½ teaspoons fast-action dried yeast
1 teaspoon sea salt
⅔ cups/160 ml warm water
2 balls of burrata cheese, torn into small pieces
12 slices of prosciutto
6 figs, quartered
4 red Serrano chiles/chillies, sliced
extra virgin olive oil, for oiling the bowl
all-purpose/plain flour, for dusting
oil, for brushing the grate
truffle honey, for drizzling

MAKES 6

Flatbreads are such a fun way to start a party. They are quick to cook on the grill and guests can nibble on them while the rest of the meal comes together. The combination of figs and prosciutto is a wonderful marriage of sweet and salty flavors. Pick up some flatbreads from your local store if you want to reduce the prep time.

Oil a large bowl and set aside.

Place the flour, yeast, and salt in the bowl of a food processor. With the motor running, add the warm water to the flour mixture in a steady stream until all the liquid is incorporated and the dough forms a ball–this will take about 3 minutes.

Place the dough on a floured worktop and knead to form a ball. Place in the oiled bowl and cover with a kitchen towel. Set aside in a warm place for about 3 hours to double in size.

Heat the grill/barbecue to medium-high. Brush the grate with oil.

Remove the dough from the bowl and cut into six pieces. Roll each piece out into a circle.

Place the dough on the hot grill and cook for about 3-5 minutes until golden and charred. Using a pair of tongs, turn the flatbreads over. Top each crust with some burrata, two slices of prosciutto, and four pieces of fig. Sprinkle with the Serrano chiles/chillies.

Close the lid and cook for 5 minutes until the cheese has melted, the prosciutto is crispy, and the flatbreads are charred and crusty.

To serve, remove from the grill to a wooden board and drizzle with a little truffle honey.

DESSERTS & SWEET BAKES

ROASTED STRAWBERRY & GINGER SEMIFREDDO

20 strawberries (about 1 lb./450 g), quartered
½ cup/100 g superfine/caster sugar, plus 2 tablespoons
3 tablespoons finely chopped stem ginger
3 large (UK medium) eggs
2 large (UK medium) egg yolks
2 cups/500 g heavy/double whipping cream

a 10 x 4-inch/25 x 10-cm loaf pan, lined with plastic wrap/clingfilm

SERVES 6-8

Roasting the strawberries as this gives them a deep, lush, rich, and intense flavor, which bursts with summer sunshine. Use stem ginger to give a gentle tang to the custard. You can turn the semifreddo out onto a large plate and slice to serve, or scoop into bowls—either way will give you a dramatic and eye-catching dessert.

Preheat the oven to 425°F (220°C) Gas 7.

Place the strawberries, 2 tablespoons of sugar, and the ginger in a food processor and pulse into a chunky sauce. Pour the mixture into a ceramic baking dish and roast in the preheated oven for 20 minutes. Remove from the oven and cool (this can be made a day ahead if you wish).

In a heatproof bowl whisk together the eggs, egg yolks, and remaining sugar until just blended, then place over a saucepan of simmering water. Using an electric hand mixer, beat for 4 minutes. Remove from the heat and continue to beat for another 4 minutes until the mixture is thick and frothy. Set aside.

Pour the cream into the bowl of an electric stand mixer and beat until soft peaks form. Fold in the custard mixture until combined.

Pour a third of the cooled strawberry sauce into the prepared loaf pan and cover with a third of the custard mixture. Continue to layer twice more.

Place a piece of baking parchment on top of the semifreddo, then cover with foil and freeze for 6 hours until firm.

PERFUMED POACHED PEACHES

4 sweet firm ripe peaches
Elderflower Poaching Wine
   (see page 176)
small edible flowers, to garnish
   (optional)
mascarpone, to serve

SERVES 4

A stunningly beautiful dessert, filled with simplicity and heady aromatics for a hot summer evening. It is lovely served chilled with a sprinkling of tiny edible flowers or even some herbs—whatever you have in the garden.

Put the peaches in a non-reactive pan and pour over the Elderflower Poaching Wine. Bring to the boil over medium-high heat, then reduce to a lively simmer and cook for 8–10 minutes—you want the peaches to be cooked but still hold their shape. Remove the peaches with a slotted spoon, put on a plate, and set aside to cool.

Increase the heat under the pan and simmer the poaching liquid to reduce by half—this should take about 5 minutes—then turn off the heat and allow to cool.

Peel the peaches and place each one in a bowl. Drizzle with the cooled syrup. Sprinkle with flowers, if using, and serve with mascarpone.

COOK'S NOTE: You can chill the peaches and syrup in the fridge until ready to serve—this can be made a day ahead.

VIN SANTO GRILLED PEACHES

4 firm ripe peaches
8 tablespoons honey or honeycomb
1 bottle of Vin Santo
1 tablespoon finely chopped sage
oil, for brushing the grate
crème fraîche or sour cream, to serve

SERVES 4

Peach season never lasts long enough! Plump, ripe, sweet, juicy peaches can be cut up and tossed into salads, made into ice cream and tarts, or simply eaten just as they are with good cheese. Here the peaches are soaked in Vin Santo, then grilled over mesquite embers until charred and caramelized. Enjoy with a small glass of Vin Santo.

Heat the grill/barbecue to medium-high. Brush the grate with oil.

Cut the peaches in half and remove the pits/stones. Lay the peaches cut-side down on the grill and cook for 3–4 minutes, then turn them over using a pair of tongs.

Place a tablespoon of honey or honeycomb in the center of each peach half, then fill with Vin Santo. Sprinkle the peach halves with the chopped sage. Cook for another 5 minutes until caramelized and slightly charred.

Serve with crème fraîche or sour cream and a small glass of Vin Santo.

GOAT CHEESE ICE CREAM

WITH GRILLED HONEY FIGS

4 egg yolks
2 tablespoons granulated sugar
2 cups/500 ml goat milk or
    whole milk
1 cup/250 ml heavy/double cream
½ cup/125 ml honey
8 oz./225 g goat cheese, at
    room temperature, crumbled
pinch of kosher salt
10 ripe black figs, halved and
    stems removed
½ teaspoon ground cardamom
oil, for brushing the grate

SERVES 6-8

Fig season arrives at the height of summer when the days are long and the sun is hot. Grilling the figs infuses them with a wonderfully rich, charred caramel flavor.

Whisk together the egg yolks and sugar in a medium-sized bowl and set aside.

Heat the milk, cream, and half of the honey in a saucepan over a medium-high heat until just below boiling point. Slowly pour the hot milk mixture over the eggs, whisking continuously, then pour the mixture back into the saucepan. Continue to cook over low-medium heat, stirring continuously until the custard is thick and coats the back of a wooden spoon.

Pour the custard into a blender, add the goat cheese and salt, and blend until smooth. Cover and cool in the fridge for 2-24 hours.

Freeze the custard in an ice cream maker according to the manufacturer's instructions. Store in an airtight container in the freezer until ready to serve.

Place the figs in a ceramic bowl, add the remaining honey and the cardamom, and toss to coat the figs all over. Set aside for 30 minutes to marinate.

Heat the grill/barbecue to medium-high. Brush the grate with oil.

Grill the figs for about 4 minutes on each side until caramelized and slightly charred. Return the cooked figs to the bowl that they were marinating in, so they can soak up any excess juices. Cover and set aside.

To serve, scoop the ice cream into bowls and top with the grilled figs.

GRILLED BANANA BOATS

7 oz/200 g bittersweet/dark chocolate, 72% cocoa solids
2 tablespoons maple syrup
2 tablespoons/30 g butter
¾ cup/180 ml heavy/double cream
pinch of ground cinnamon
pinch of salt
6 bananas
1 quart/1 litre coffee ice cream
1 cup/225 g candied pecans, crushed
oil, for brushing the grate

SERVES 6

An old-fashioned dessert from the diner, cooked on the grill and transformed into a wonderful caramelized dessert. Top with coffee ice cream and dark chocolate sauce, sprinkle with nuts, and dig in.

Heat the grill/barbecue to medium–high. Brush the grate with oil.

To make the chocolate sauce, place the chocolate, maple syrup, butter, cream, cinnamon, and salt in a pan over medium heat. Stir the mixture continuously until the chocolate has melted and you have a smooth sauce. Pour into a small pitcher/jug and set aside.

Place the unpeeled bananas on the grill and cook for 3–4 minutes, then turn them over and continue to cook for another 5 minutes until the skins are charred.

Remove the bananas from the grill. Using a sharp knife, make a slit in the peel from top to bottom and open out slightly. Top each banana with a scoop of ice cream, pour over some chocolate sauce, and sprinkle with the pecans.

SPICY DARK CHOCOLATE & COCONUT POTS

12 oz./340 g bittersweet/dark
   chocolate, 72% cocoa solids,
   finely chopped
2 teaspoons ground Ancho chili/chilli
   powder
½ teaspoon ground cinnamon
2 x 14-oz/400-ml cans of coconut milk
chocolate shavings, to decorate

SERVES 6

These dark little chocolate pots are a dream to eat and a dream to make. This is a simple recipe that can be whisked up quickly and ahead of time, which leaves you more time with your guests. Ancho chili powder is used here to add a little kick, but you can use any kind of spice to give it an extra flavor dimension.

Break up the chocolate and place in a large bowl. Add the chili/chilli powder and cinnamon.

In a medium-sized saucepan bring the coconut milk to the boil over a medium–high heat. Pour the hot milk over the chocolate and stir until it has completely melted.

Pour the chocolate mixture into six small bowls or ramekins. Cover and place in the fridge for about 1½ hours until set.

When ready to serve, remove from the fridge and grate a little chocolate over each pot.

MATCHA ICE CREAM

WITH BLACK SESAME PRALINE

2 cups/500 ml whole milk
2 tablespoons powdered
   matcha green tea
1 cup/250 ml heavy/double cream
¾ cup/150 g superfine/caster sugar
6 egg yolks

PRALINE
1 tablespoon toasted sesame oil
1½ cups/300 g superfine/caster sugar
½ cup/70 g black sesame seeds

SERVES 6-8

Delicious green tea ice cream with sweet crunchy sesame praline is a feast for the eyes! Matcha is green tea that has been ground into a powder which dissolves quickly in either hot or cold water to make a refreshing drink. Add it to cake mixtures and smoothies, or sprinkle over ceviche.

In a small bowl whisk together ⅓ cup/80 ml of the milk and the matcha powder and let sit for 5 minutes.

Pour the remaining milk into a saucepan, whisk in the cream and matcha mix, and then cook over medium heat until just below boiling point.

In a medium-sized bowl whisk together the sugar and egg yolks. Slowly pour in the hot milk, whisking continuously, then pour back into the saucepan. Stir over low heat until the mixture is thick and coats the back of a wooden spoon. Set aside to cool to room temperature, then place in the fridge for 4 hours.

Freeze the chilled custard in an ice cream maker according to the manufacturer's instructions. Store in an airtight container in the freezer until ready to use.

To make the praline, brush a baking sheet with the sesame oil and set aside. Place the sugar in a saucepan with ⅓ cup/80 ml water over high heat and cook for 6-8 minutes until dark golden brown. Do not stir.

Pour evenly over the prepared baking sheet and sprinkle with the sesame seeds. Set aside to harden. Break into chunks and serve with scoops of the ice cream.

BOURBON RAISIN ICE CREAM SANDWICHES

1 cup/100 g raisins/sultanas,
   golden or dark or mixed
1 cup/250 ml bourbon
4 egg yolks
½ cup/100 g turbinado sugar
2 cups/500 ml whole milk
1 cup/250 ml heavy/double cream
pinch of kosher salt
Chocolate Chip Cookies (see page 160)

SERVES 10

Velvety ice cream laced with rum-soaked raisins and sandwiched between decadent chocolate cookies is a great way for grown-ups to end a barbecue. Keep a supply of dried fruits soaked in liquor in the pantry—they make fabulous additions to ice creams and desserts.

Place the raisins/sultanas in a bowl and cover with the bourbon. Set aside to soak for 6–24 hours until the raisins have plumped up.

Strain the raisins and reserve the bourbon, which should yield about ½ cup/125 ml depending on how long you soaked them for.

Whisk the egg yolks, sugar, and bourbon together in a medium-sized bowl and set aside.

Heat the milk and cream together in a saucepan over medium–high heat until just below boiling point. Slowly pour the hot milk over the egg mixture, whisking continuously, then pour the mixture back into the saucepan.

Continue to cook over low–medium heat, stirring continuously, until the custard is thick and coats the back of a wooden spoon.

Cover and cool in the fridge for 4 hours, then freeze the custard in an ice cream maker according to the manufacturer's instructions. When the desired consistency is reached, add the raisins for 2–3 turns of the paddle.

To make the ice cream sandwiches, lay ten cookies on a baking sheet and top with a scoop of ice cream. Top with remaining cookies and gently press together to make a sandwich. Individually wrap the sandwiches in plastic wrap/clingfilm and store in the freezer until ready to eat.

GRILLED DONUT S'MORES

WITH CHILE CHOCOLATE SAUCE

7 oz./200 g bittersweet/dark chocolate, 72% cocoa solids
2 tablespoons maple syrup
2 teaspoons butter
¾ cup/180 ml heavy/double cream
1½ teaspoons ground cinnamon
½ teaspoon Ancho chili/chilli powder
½ teaspoon smoked paprika
24 marshmallows
6 donuts, cut in half horizontally
oil, for brushing the grate

SERVES 6

An all-out extravaganza of caramelized sugar, s'mores are one of those desserts that have no rules. Have fun by wrapping the marshmallows up in donuts, then toasting them and dunking them in a wonderful spice-infused chocolate sauce. Instead of donuts, you could also use cronuts or cookies.

To make the chocolate sauce, break up the chocolate and place in a medium-sized pan along with the maple syrup, butter, cream, cinnamon, chili/chilli powder, and paprika. Stirring continuously, cook over low–medium heat until the chocolate has melted and you have a smooth sauce. Set aside.

Line a baking sheet with half of the the donut halves. Place four marshmallows on each of these, then top with the other halves. Press gently together to sandwich them together.

Heat the grill/barbecue to medium–high. Brush the grate with oil.

Lay the doughnuts on the grill and cook for about 1 minute on each side until brown and slightly charred.

Serve with the warm chocolate sauce for either drizzling or dunking.

GRILLED PEACH MELBA

6 ripe firm peaches
¼ cup/60 ml orange blossom honey
2 tablespoons turbinado sugar
2¾ cups/350 g raspberries
¼ cup/60 g superfine/caster sugar
1 teaspoon freshly squeezed
    lemon juice
a few drops of rosewater
1 quart/1 litre good-quality vanilla
    ice cream
oil, for brushing the grate
edible flowers, to decorate (optional)

SERVES 6

This is such a ubiquitous British dessert, invented at the Savoy Hotel in London by Escoffier to celebrate the Australian soprano Nellie Melba. He poached the peaches, but here they are cooked on a hot grill to release all their sweetness. Make life easy and pick a really good local artisanal vanilla ice cream.

Cut the peaches in half, discard the pits/stones, and place cut-side up in a ceramic dish. Drizzle with the honey, sprinkle with the turbinado sugar, and set aside.

Place the raspberries, superfine/caster sugar, and lemon juice in a blender and process to a smooth sauce. Stir in a few drops of rosewater and pour into a pitcher/jug.

Heat the grill/barbecue to medium-high. Brush the grate with oil.

Lay the peaches cut-side down on the grill and cook for 3-4 minutes until they are caramelized and slightly charred. Turn them over and continue to cook for another 3-4 minutes.

For each person, place two peach halves on a plate and top with a scoop of vanilla ice cream. Drizzle with the raspberry sauce and serve, decorated with edible flowers if you wish.

SOZZLED APRICOT BRUSCHETTA

1½ lb./680 g (about 18) ripe apricots, halved and pitted
Italian Dessert Poaching Wine (see page 177)
6 slices panettone or brioche, about 1½ inches/4 cm thick
Orange Cream (see below)
honey, for drizzling

SERVES 6

This is a show stopper. Grilled panettone topped with sozzled apricots, lavishly dolloped with orange cream and a decadent drizzle of honey. It is the most delicious dessert to serve when apricots are in season. If there are any leftover sozzled apricots, store in the fridge and have with cheeses or stir into yogurt.

Put the apricot halves in a non-reactive pan and add the Italian Dessert Poaching Wine. Set the pan over medium-high heat and bring to the boil, then reduce the heat to medium-low and simmer for 10 minutes. You want the apricots to cook but still hold a little of their shape.

Remove the apricots from the pan with a slotted spoon and put in a ceramic bowl. Turn the heat back up to medium-high and simmer for about 5 minutes to reduce the poaching liquid by half, stirring frequently. Pour the syrup over the apricots.

Heat a grill/barbecue to medium-high heat, or place a grill pan on the stove top over medium-high heat.

Grill the panettone or brioche slices for about 2 minutes per side, until toasted. Place each one on a plate and spoon the sozzled apricots, along with the juices, over each slice of toasted panettone. Dollop with the orange cream, drizzle with honey, and serve.

ORANGE CREAM

1 cup/240 ml crème fraîche
grated zest of 1 orange
1 tablespoon orange blossom honey
3 tablespoons orange liqueur, such as Grand Mariner or Cointreau

YIELDS 1¼ CUPS/300 ML

Flavoring creams and yogurts can add a delicious layer to desserts. You can use fruits, spices, herbs, and wines to do it. Just have fun experimenting. You will not be disappointed.

Put all the ingredients in a glass bowl and whisk together. Cover and refrigerate until ready to use.

Store the cream in the refrigerator for up to 1 week.

Serve on the side of desserts, such as tarts and poached fruits, or with scones and breads.

LEMONGRASS SUMMER BERRIES

4 cups/500 g raspberries
2 cups/230 g strawberries
Lemongrass Poaching Syrup (see
  page 176)
lemon verbena, to garnish (optional)
Rose Cream (see below), to serve

SERVES 4-6

Nothing in the world shouts 'summer' better than fresh strawberries and raspberries. Picked sweet and juicy they need very little to dress them up. Lemongrass perfumes the fruits and the floral rose cream turns the dish into a bouquet of flavors.

Rinse the berries under cold water and hull the strawberries.

Put the berries in a serving dish and pour over the lemongrass syrup. Allow to marinate for 1-4 hours.

Garnish with lemon verbena and serve with lots of Rose Cream.

ROSE CREAM

1 cup/240 ml heavy/double cream
1 tablespoon granulated/caster sugar
a few drops of rosewater

YIELDS 1 CUP/240 ML

Rosewater is a dreamy essence that is used a lot in Middle Eastern cooking. It perfumes food with a wonderful tone. Here it is used to infuse cream, which you can dollop on desserts, such as the Lemongrass Summer Berries above, or serve with scones and jam for afternoon tea.

Pour the cream into a bowl and beat with an electric hand whisk until thickened. Fold in the sugar, add a few drops of rosewater, and stir to combine. Cover and refrigerate until ready to use.

CHILLED PEAR YOGURT

3 pears, cored, skin on
32 oz./950 ml plain full-fat yogurt
2 tablespoons honey
2 cups ice cubes
a pinch of salt
Pickled Rose Petals (see below),
   to garnish

SERVES 6-8

This is a bright and lively soup, which is lovely served in small glasses as an appetizer. Adding the Pickled Rose Petals (see below) not only makes it look gorgeous, but also complements the gentle taste of the pears.

Place all the ingredients apart from the Pickled Rose Petals in a food processor and blend until smooth. Pour into glasses filled with ice and top with the Pickled Rose Petals. Serve immediately.

COOKS' NOTE: Replace the pears with apples, nectarines, or peaches, depending on what is in season.

PICKLED ROSE PETALS

petals of 8 small edible roses
   (about 3 cups/60 g petals), rinsed
2 cups/475 ml champagne vinegar or
   white wine vinegar
2 drops rose water (optional)

MAKES 4 CUPS/950 ML

What in life is better than champagne and roses? These pretty pickled petals make any dish or drink look glamorous and add a wonderfully heady floral flavor.

Place the rose petals in a ceramic bowl.

Put the champagne vinegar into a non-reactive pan over low heat and warm through. Take care not to boil the vinegar as it will damage the delicate petals. Remove from the heat and add the rose water. Cool for 5 minutes, then pour over the petals. Cover and leave to pickle overnight.

COOKS' NOTE: To make rose petal vinegar, leave the rose petals in the vinegar in cool, dark place or a refrigerator for 5 days–1 month. Strain through cheesecloth/muslin and store in sterilized glass bottles.

ROULADE
WITH PROVENÇAL PEACHES

4 large (UK medium) eggs
½ cup/100 g golden granulated/
    caster sugar
2 tablespoons melted butter
½ teaspoon kosher/rock salt
1 cup/125 g cake/plain flour, sifted
6 Provençal Peaches (see page 175),
    drained with syrup reserved,
    and sliced
1½ cups/225 g raspberries
confectioners'/icing sugar, for dusting
crème fraîche, to serve

*a 13 x 9-inch/33 x 23-cm baking sheet,
    lined with baking parchment and
    lightly sprayed with vegetable oil*

SERVES 6-8

Update the classic jelly/jam Swiss roll into a ridiculously delicious dessert by adding your homemade bottled fruit. You can mix and match fruits and flavor creams, and freeze the roulade to serve it as a frozen dessert.

Preheat the oven to 375°F (190°C) Gas 5.

Whisk together the eggs and sugar for 5-6 minutes until pale and fluffy. Pour in the melted butter, add the salt, and stir to combine. Slowly fold in the flour and pour the batter onto the prepared baking sheet. Spread out evenly, and bake for 10-12 minutes until golden and springy.

Remove from the oven and set aside for a few minutes. Sprinkle a clean kitchen towel with confectioners'/icing sugar. Invert the cake onto the towel and remove the parchment from the base. Beginning with the short sides, roll the cake up in the towel and leave to cool for 2 hours.

Place the reserved peach syrup in a small pan, bring to the boil, and cook until reduced by half.

Unroll the cake and remove the kitchen towel. Spread crème fraîche evenly over the cake. Toss the sliced peaches and raspberries together in a bowl and arrange on top of the cake, then roll it up tightly.

Place the cake seam-side down on a serving platter. Dust with confectioners'/icing sugar and serve with the warm syrup.

COOKS' NOTE: This recipe works well with any bottled fruits.

FRANGIPANE TART

WITH VIN SANTO PLUMS

1 lb./450 g ready-made shortcrust
  pastry
1 cup/100 g finely ground almonds
1 stick/115 g butter, softened
½ cup/100 g superfine/caster sugar
2 eggs, lightly beaten
2 tablespoons all-purpose/plain flour,
  plus extra for dusting
2 teaspoons baking powder
¼ teaspoon pure vanilla extract
1 tablespoon amaretto or other
  almond liqueur
Vin Santo Plum Spoon Fruit (see page
  175), pitted/stoned

*2 rectangular tart pans or a 10-inch/
25-cm round tart pan, greased*

SERVES 6-8

Frangipane is a complete crowd-pleaser for any occasion. Toasting the almonds gives the tart a nutty, rich flavor. You can make it in a rectangular pan (as pictured) or round, either way it's always great.

Roll out the pastry on a lightly floured surface into a large rectangle. Press the pastry into the prepared tart pan and trim the edges. Using a fork prick the base of the tart all over. Cover with plastic wrap/clingfilm and return to the refrigerator for 30 minutes.

Preheat the oven to 350°F (175°C) Gas 4.

Toast the ground almonds over medium heat until golden. Set aside.

In an electric stand mixer cream together the butter and sugar until light and fluffy. Slowly add the eggs and beat until combined. Add the flour, baking powder, pure vanilla extract, and amaretto, and continue to beat until completely mixed. Stir in the ground almonds.

Pour the frangipane mixture into the pastry shell and top with Vin Santo Plums—as many as you want. Bake in the preheated oven for 45 minutes, until the mixture has risen, and is golden and firm to the touch. It will puff up while cooking but then sinks a little when cooling. Remove from the oven and cool for 10 minutes.

In a small pan heat the Vin Santo Plum syrup. Drizzle the warm syrup over the tart and serve.

SUMMER FRUIT & AMARETTO COBBLER

6 ripe firm nectarines
10 ripe firm apricots
1½ cups/150 g blueberries
1½ cups/150 g blackberries
⅔ cup/150 g coconut sugar
1 tablespoon cornstarch/cornflour
¼ cup/60 ml amaretto
4 tablespoons/60 g cold
   unsalted butter, cubed
1½ cups/210 g unbleached
   all-purpose/plain flour
1 tablespoon baking powder
4 tablespoons dark brown sugar
pinch of sea salt
1 cup/250 ml heavy/double cream
¼ cup/30 g chopped almonds
vanilla ice cream, to serve

a 12-inch/30-cm cast-iron pan

SERVES 6

Cobblers are a favorite with everyone. Tinged with a little old-fashioned familiarity, they make the most wonderful summer desserts. Mix and match berries and stone fruit, or keep it simple with just one kind. Serve warm with lashings of ice cream. You can easily cook this on a barbecue—just set the pan over indirect heat and close the lid.

Preheat the oven to 375°F (190°C) Gas 5 or heat the grill/barbecue to medium-high.

Cut the nectarines and apricots in half and remove the pits/stones. Slice the fruit into ½-inch/1-cm thick wedges and place in a large ceramic bowl. Add the blueberries, blackberries, coconut sugar, cornstarch/cornflour, and half the amaretto and stir, making sure all the fruit is evenly coated. Set aside to marinate for 30 minutes.

Place the butter, flour, baking powder, 2 tablespoons of the brown sugar, and the salt in the bowl of a food processor and pulse until the mixture resembles breadcrumbs. With the motor running, add the remaining amaretto and cream and process until the mixture forms a dough.

Pour the fruit mixture into the cast-iron pan. Using a dessertspoon, drop spoonfuls of the cobbler mix on top of the fruit, then sprinkle with the remaining sugar and the chopped almonds.

Bake in the preheated oven for 30–35 minutes until the cobbler is golden brown and the fruit is bubbling. If using the grill, place the pan on indirect heat, close the lid, and cook for about 20 minutes.

Serve with vanilla ice cream.

BLACKBERRY & PISTACHIO CAKE
WITH LIME SYRUP

2 cups/260 g all-purpose/plain flour
1 tablespoon baking powder
⅔ cup/150 g unsalted butter, softened, plus extra for greasing
1 cup/200 g superfine/caster sugar
3 large (UK medium) eggs, at room temperature
1 cup/225 g full-fat Greek yogurt
¼ cup/1 oz salted pistachios, finely ground
1 cup/100 g blackberries, roughly chopped

LIME SYRUP
1½ cups/300 g granulated/caster sugar
grated zest of 4 limes
1 cup/250 ml freshly squeezed lime juice (about 4 large limes)

a 10-inch/25-cm cake pan with a removable base, base-lined with baking parchment, then base and sides greased with butter

SERVES 8-10

You can dress this cake up by piling lots of fresh berries on top with a few blackberry leaves and a dusting of powdered sugar or simply leave as is. Either serve it warm with homemade vanilla ice cream, or make it a day ahead, drizzle with zesty lime syrup, and let sit overnight for the flavors to meld, then serve with a large dollop of crème fraîche.

Preheat the oven to 350°F (175°C) Gas 4.

Sift the flour and baking powder together into a bowl and set aside.

In the bowl of a stand mixer fitted with a paddle, cream the butter and sugar for about 5 minutes until light and fluffy. Add the eggs one at a time and beat until smooth. Add the yogurt and continue to beat.

Reduce the speed and slowly add the flour mixture, beating until well combined. Add the pistachios and stir to mix completely.

Remove the bowl from the stand mixer and stir in the blackberries with one or two turns of the spoon until just mixed—you don't want the batter to turn pink.

Pour into the prepared cake pan and bake in the preheated oven for 1 hour until golden brown and a thin skewer inserted into the center comes out clean.

Remove the cake from the oven and place on a wire rack. Pierce the top all over with a skewer and cool in the pan for 20 minutes.

To make the syrup, place the sugar, zest, and lime juice in a small pan. Bring to the boil over medium-high heat, stirring to dissolve the sugar. Cook for about 5 minutes until it becomes a light syrup. Drizzle the lime syrup over the cooled cake, then loosely cover and leave overnight before serving.

CHOCOLATE CHIP COOKIES

2 cups/260 g all-purpose/plain flour
½ cup/40 g cocoa powder, plus
   extra for dusting
½ teaspoon baking powder
½ teaspoon baking soda/bicarbonate
   of soda
pinch of kosher salt
12 oz/340 g bittersweet/dark chocolate,
   72% cocoa solids, finely chopped
¾ cup/170 g unsalted butter, softened
1 cup/210 g dark brown sugar
1 large (UK medium) egg

*3 baking sheets lined with baking
   parchment*

MAKES 20

Decadent dark chocolate cookies must be a pantry staple—perfect to sandwich homemade ice cream between them (see page 139).

Preheat the oven to 350°F (175°C) Gas 4.

Sift together the flour, cocoa powder, baking powder, baking soda/bicarbonate of soda, and salt and set aside.

Melt 4 oz/115 g of the chopped chocolate either in a bowl set over a saucepan of simmering water or in a microwave. Let cool slightly.

In the bowl of a stand mixer fitted with the paddle attachment, cream together the butter and sugar on medium-high speed for about 4 minutes until light and fluffy. Beat in the egg until combined, then slowly pour in the cooled melted chocolate.

Reduce the speed to slow and add the flour mixture a little at a time until combined, scraping down the sides of the mixer bowl as needed. Remove the bowl from the stand and stir in the remaining chopped chocolate. Cover the bowl and refrigerate for 5 minutes.

Using a small 2-inch/5-cm ice cream scoop or large spoon, drop the dough onto the prepared baking sheets, spacing them 4 inches/10 cm apart.

With the palm of your hand, press the dough down into 3-inch/7.5-cm circles, approx. ½ inch/1 cm thick. Cover and place in the freezer for 10 minutes.

Bake in the preheated oven for 15 minutes, then remove to a cooling rack. When cool, dust with cocoa powder.

THE PANTRY

BLISTERED JALAPEÑO, LIME, & TEQUILA RELISH

3 tablespoons olive oil, plus extra
  for oiling
4 jalapeño chiles/chillies
1 red and 1 white onion, thinly sliced
3 garlic cloves, finely chopped
skin of 1 Pickled Makrut Lime
  (see page 170), finely diced
2 tablespoons tequila
3 tablespoons clear honey
¼ cup/60 ml white wine vinegar
sea salt

*still-warm sterilized glass jars
  with airtight lids*

MAKES 2 CUPS/475 ML

Once you taste this divine relish you will be dolloping it on everything you eat! Roasting the jalapeños and blistering the skins sweetens them and picks out a smoky flavor. Enjoy with the Grilled Halloumi on page 24.

Place a lightly oiled large cast-iron pan over high heat until smoking. Add the jalapeños, lower the heat slightly, and cook until the skins are charred and blistered. Remove from the pan and set aside to cool.

Add the oil, sliced onions, and garlic to the pan and cook over medium heat for 5 minutes, stirring occasionally. Season with salt to taste. Add the diced lime skin with the onion.

Roughly chop the cooled jalapeños and add to the pan along with the tequila, honey, and vinegar. Cook for a further 10 minutes, until the onions are golden brown and soft.

Pack the relish into warm sterilized glass jars, leaving a ½-inch/5-mm space at the top, and carefully tap the jars on the counter to get rid of any air pockets. Wipe the jars clean and screw on the lids. Seal the jars for 10 minutes following the Water Bath Method (see page 4). Once sealed, store unopened in a cool, dark place for up to 12 months.

COOKS' NOTE: You can substitute the jalapeños for any kind of fresh chile/chilli.

PROVENÇAL OLIVE RELISH

2 cups/200 g pitted/stoned Kalamata
    olives, drained
12 anchovy fillets
¼ cup/40 g capers
grated zest and juice of 1 lemon
¼ cup/60 ml extra virgin olive oil,
    plus extra to cover
cracked black pepper

sterilized glass jars with airtight lids

MAKES 3 CUPS/700 ML

This is Provence in a jar! The olives are drenched in oil and spiced with capers and salty anchovies. It works perfectly on bruschetta, pizzas, crudités, and pickled eggs, or lightly spread on chicken before roasting in the oven.

Place all the ingredients in a food processor and blend until the mixture is almost smooth but still has some texture. Season with pepper.

Pack the tapenade into sterilized glass jars and drizzle with a little olive oil to cover the surface. Store in the refrigerator for up to 6 months.

CORN & POBLANO RELISH

3 Poblano chiles/chillies
2 tablespoons olive oil, plus extra
    for oiling
2 garlic cloves, finely chopped
1 red onion, finely diced
1 red (bell) pepper, finely diced
3 ears of corn, kernels removed
    (approximately 3 cups/420 g kernels)
6 scallions/spring onions, thinly sliced
grated zest and freshly squeezed juice
    of 1 lime
1 tablespoon Aleppo pepper/Turkish
    chilli flakes
¾ cup/150 g light brown sugar
1¾ cups/425 ml apple cider vinegar
sea salt and cracked black pepper

*still-warm sterilized glass jars
    with airtight lids*

MAKES 2 CUPS/475 ML

This relish is sweet and tangy and has a lot of spice. Delicious spooned over tacos, burgers, hot dogs, and any kind of grilled foods.

Place a lightly oiled large cast-iron pan over high heat until smoking. Add the Poblano chiles/chillies, lower the heat slightly, and cook until the skins are charred and blistered. Remove from the pan and set aside to cool.

Once cool, roughly chop the Poblano chiles and set aside. Return the pan to medium heat and add the olive oil, garlic, red onion, and (bell) pepper, and sauté for 5 minutes. Add the chopped Poblanos, corn kernels, scallions/spring onions, lime zest and juice, and Aleppo pepper, and stir. Add the sugar, pour in the vinegar, and season with salt and pepper. Stir and bring to the boil, then reduce the heat and simmer for 15–20 minutes.

Pack the relish into warm sterilized glass jars, leaving a ½-inch/5-mm space at the top. Carefully tap the jars on the counter top to get rid of air pockets. Wipe the jars clean and screw on the lids.

Seal the jars for 10 minutes following the Water Bath Method (see page 4). Once sealed, store unopened in a cool, dark place for up to 12 months.

HARICOTS VERTS

WITH PICKLED ONIONS

1 lb./450 g haricots verts
  (green beans), trimmed
1 lb./450 g pickled cocktail onions,
  drained and brine reserved
6 bay leaves
½ cup/125 ml red wine vinegar
1 tablespoon peppercorns
2 tablespoons piri piri rub
  (see Cooks' Note)
2 tablespoons brown sugar
2 tablespoons brown mustard seeds

sterilized glass jars with airtight lids

MAKES 4 CUPS/950 ML

Peeling pounds of tiny onions for bottling can be boring and fussy, so using pre-pickled onions as a shortcut here is a clever cheat.

Pack the haricots verts, cocktail onions, and bay leaves into sterilized glass jars, leaving a ½-inch/1-cm space at the top.

In a non-reactive pan, bring the brine from the onions, vinegar, 3 cups (700 ml) cold water, peppercorns, piri piri rub, sugar, and mustard seeds to a boil over medium–high heat. Reduce the heat and simmer for about 8 minutes, until the sugar has dissolved.

Pour the brine over the packed vegetables and carefully tap the jars on the counter top to get rid of air pockets. Screw on the lids. Seal the jars for 10 minutes following the Water Bath Method (see page 4). Once sealed, store unopened in a cool, dark place for up to 12 months.

COOKS' NOTE: To make your own piri piri rub, mix together 1 tablespoon red pepper flakes/dried chilli flakes, 1 tablespoon smoked paprika, and 1 tablespoon tomato powder.

GARDEN PATCH PICKLES

bunch of radishes, halved lengthwise
bunch of baby carrots
½ cup/50 g pickled cornichons/
  mini gherkins
1 garlic clove, thinly sliced
3 celery stalks, cut in thirds
1 red onion, sliced
4 Persian cucumbers, quartered
bunch of pencil-thin asparagus
4 cups/950 ml red wine vinegar
½ cup/110 g brown sugar
1 tablespoon mustard seeds
1 tablespoon fennel seeds
1 tablespoon cumin seeds
1 tablespoon dried rosemary

sterilized glass jars with airtight lids

MAKES 8 CUPS/1.8 L

The name Garden Patch refers to the fact that these ingredients are very standard vegetables that work really well together when pickled. They stand up to strong spices and make nice, crunchy pickles to serve with Rillettes (see page 12), charcuterie, and cheese.

Pack all the vegetables into sterilized, size-appropriate glass jars leaving ½-inch/1-cm space at the top.

Put the vinegar, sugar, mustard seeds, fennel seeds, cumin seeds, and dried rosemary in a non-reactive pan and bring to the boil over medium heat. Turn down the heat and stir for 8–10 minutes until the sugar has dissolved.

Pour the hot vinegar mixture over the vegetables and carefully tap the jars on the counter to get rid of any air pockets. Wipe the jars clean and tightly screw on the lids. Turn the jars upside down and leave until completely cooled.

Store in the refrigerator for at least 24 hours before serving. The pickles can be stored in the refrigerator for up to 2 months.

PICKLED GREEN TOMATOES

3 cups/700 ml apple cider vinegar
¾ cup/150 g turbinado/demerara
    sugar
1½ teaspoons mustard seeds
1½ teaspoons green peppercorns
4 large green tomatoes, quartered
    or sliced
2 garlic stalks, cut in half lengthwise

*still-warm sterilized glass jars
    with airtight lids*

MAKES 8 CUPS/1.8 L

In springtime when fresh garlic starts appearing at the farmers' market so, too, do the season's first green tomatoes. The two are a pickle dream.

Put the vinegar, sugar, mustard seeds, and green peppercorns in a non-reactive pan and bring to the boil over medium heat. Turn down the heat and stir for 8–10 minutes until the sugar has dissolved.

Pack the tomatoes and garlic into warm, sterilized, size-appropriate glass jars, leaving a ½-inch/1-cm space at the top. Pour over the hot vinegar mixture and carefully tap the jars on the counter to get rid of any air pockets. Wipe the jars clean and screw on the lids. Seal the jars for 10 minutes following the Water Bath Method (see page 4).

Once sealed, store unopened in a cool, dark place for up to 12 months.

COOKS' NOTE: To quick seal, screw on the lids and turn the jars upside down to cool completely, then store in the refrigerator for up to 2 months.

PICKLED MAKRUT LIMES

24 small makrut limes, quartered
12 makrut lime leaves
2 cups/475 ml rice wine vinegar
2 tablespoons granulated/caster sugar
1 tablespoon kosher/rock salt

*still-warm sterilized glass jars
    with airtight lids*

MAKES 8 CUPS/1.8 L

Keep the pickling solution simple, as you want the wonderful floral aroma of the makrut limes and leaves to sing. Add to crab cakes (see page 19), pad thai, and anything you can think of—they are delicious!

Pack the limes into warm, sterilized, size-appropriate glass jars, leaving a ½-inch/1-cm space at the top. Divide the makrut leaves evenly between the jars.

Put the vinegar, sugar, and salt in a non-reactive pan and bring to a boil. Reduce the heat and simmer for 5 minutes until the sugar has dissolved.

Pour the hot vinegar mixture over the limes and carefully tap the jars on the counter to get rid of any air pockets. Wipe the jars clean and tightly screw on the lids. Turn the jars upside down to seal. Leave to cool completely, then store in the refrigerator for up to 12 months.

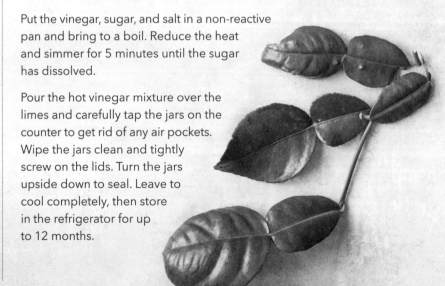

PROVENÇAL PEACHES
WITH LAVENDER

12 small firm white peaches, peeled
1½ cups/300 g superfine/caster sugar
25 oz./750 ml rosé wine
2 teaspoons edible lavender flowers

sterilized glass jars with airtight lids

MAKES 8 CUPS/1.8 L

In this dish, all the flavors of the south of France come together to brighten up a winter day when the thought of summer and the peach season is a distant memory. Eat the peaches just as they are or use them as fillings for cakes and tarts—either way, you won't be disappointed.

Place the peeled peaches whole in warm, sterilized glass jars, leaving a ½-inch/1-cm space at the top.

In a non-reactive pan, bring the sugar and wine to the boil over medium-high heat. Reduce the heat and simmer for 5 minutes until the sugar has dissolved. Remove from the heat and stir in the lavender flowers. Set aside to cool for 5 minutes. Strain the syrup through a fine-mesh strainer/sieve.

Pour the syrup over the peaches and tap the jars on the counter top to get rid of air pockets. Place a circle of parchment paper on top of the peaches to keep them submerged. Wipe the jars clean and screw on the lids. Seal the jars for 10 minutes following the Water Bath Method (see page 4).

Once sealed, store unopened in a cool, dark place for up to 12 months.

VIN SANTO PLUM SPOON FRUIT

1½ cups/350 ml Vin Santo or other dessert wine
2 tablespoons freshly squeezed lemon juice
1½ cups/275 g granulated/caster sugar
16 firm plums, rinsed
6 thyme sprigs

still-warm sterilized glass jars with airtight lids

MAKES 8 CUPS/1.8 L

This recipe uses Santa Rosa plums, which are delicious and very juicy, deep red plums.

Pour the Vin Santo and lemon juice into a non-reactive pan over medium-high heat, and add the sugar. Bring to the boil, then reduce the heat and simmer for 6–8 minutes until the sugar has dissolved.

Add the plums to the pan and cook for 3 minutes. Remove the plums with a slotted spoon and pack into warm, sterilized, glass jars, leaving a ¼-inch/5-mm space at the top. Divide the thyme between the jars.

Bring the Vin Santo syrup to the boil and continue to cook for a few minutes until it has thickened and reduced a little. Pour the hot syrup over the fruit and carefully tap the jars on the counter top to get rid of air pockets. Screw on the lids. Seal the jars for 10 minutes following the Water Bath Method (see page 4).

Once sealed, store unopened in a cool, dark place for up to 12 months.

LEMONGRASS POACHING SYRUP

1 lemongrass stalk
1 cup/200 g granulated/caster sugar

MAKES 2 CUPS/500 ML

This wonderful fragrant syrup is great for all kind of fruits, homemade lemonade, and drizzling over ice creams and sorbets. You could also try flavoring the syrup with rosemary, lemon verbena, tarragon, or rose geranium—they are all delicious.

Chop the lemongrass stalk into large chunks and bruise them with the back of your knife blade to release the oils.

Put all the ingredients in a non-reactive pan with 2 cups/480 ml water and set over medium-high heat. Bring to the boil, then reduce the heat to medium-low. Simmer for about 5-8 minutes until the sugar has dissolved. Remove from the heat and allow the syrup to cool completely.

When cool, strain the syrup into an airtight container and store in the fridge for up to 2 weeks.

ELDERFLOWER POACHING WINE

1 cup/240 ml St Germain
3 bay leaves, bruised
2 large lemon verbena sprigs
2 teaspoons granulated/caster sugar

MAKES 2 CUPS/500 ML

St Germain is a French liquor made with the blossoms of elderflowers picked in the Alps. Everyone should have a bottle on their shelves. It's heavenly scented and perfect for cocktails, or add a dash to a glass of champagne. It makes poached fruits sing!

Put all the ingredients in a non-reactive pan with 3 cups/700 ml water and set over medium-high heat. Bring to a boil, then reduce the heat to medium-low and simmer for about 5-8 minutes until the sugar has dissolved. Leave to cool, then strain.

To use, follow the recipe on page 126, adjusting the cooking time up or down according to which fruits you are poaching.

ITALIAN DESSERT POACHING WINE

1 cup/240 ml good Italian dessert wine
1 vanilla bean/pod, split in half
2 teaspoons brown sugar

MAKES 1 CUP/250 ML

This recipe uses an Italian dessert wine, but you can absolutely use any kind of sweet wine, such as a Reisling. This is such a simple way to flavor fruit, especially if a little unripe. A versatile poaching wine, that can be used for any fruits.

Put all the ingredients in a non-reactive saucepan set over a medium-high heat. Bring to the boil, then immediately reduce the heat to a simmer. Cook for about 5–6 minutes until the sugar has dissolved, then leave to cool.

Store in an airtight container in the fridge for up to 1 week.

To use, follow the recipe on page 147, adjusting the cooking time up or down according to which fruits you are poaching.

DRINKS

PISCO SOUR

ice cubes
½ cup/120 ml Pisco
¼ cup/60 ml freshly squeezed
   lime juice (Key limes if possible)
2 egg whites
3 tablespoons simple syrup
   (see page 189)
dash of angostura bitters
lime wheels, to garnish

MAKES 2

The Pisco Sour originates in Lima and it could be considered Peru's national drink. Pisco—a spirit distilled from grapes—has a bright, lively flavor with grape aromatics. Invest in a good Pisco as it makes all the difference. Mixed with lime, it makes a really nice cocktail to be sipped slowly as the sun goes down.

Fill a cocktail shaker with ice and pour in the Pisco, lime juice, egg whites, and simple syrup. Shake vigorously and strain into two glasses.

Top with a dash of angostura bitters and garnish with lime wheels.

APEROL SPRITZ

crushed ice
1 bottle of prosecco
1 bottle of Aperol
splash of club soda
1 tangerine, cut into quarters
flowering herbs, such as rosemary or basil,
    or flowers such as lavender, pansies, or
    honeysuckle, to decorate

MAKES 4

APRICOT & BASIL MIMOSA

½ cup/120 ml simple syrup
    (see page 189)
4 basil leaves
8 very ripe apricots, pitted/stoned
1 bottle of champagne, chilled

SERVES 4

The Aperol Spritz has a season and that is summer. It is a fun drink that is not too powerful and very refreshing. Dress it up by adding flowering herbs from the garden.

Fill four wine glasses with crushed ice.

Pour the prosecco nearly three-quarters of the way up the glass, then add the Aperol (the ratio is three parts prosecco to two parts Aperol). Add just a splash of club soda.

Squeeze the tangerine quarters into the glasses and decorate with flowering herbs or flowers.

This is a wonderful weekend brunch drink—light and fizzy with a herbal aromatics from the basil. Make the apricot and basil purée ahead of time (store it in the fridge for up to 24 hours) and when guests arrive all you have to do is add the chilled champagne.

In a small saucepan bring the simple syrup and basil to the boil over medium-high heat. Remove the pan from the heat and let the syrup cool, allowing the basil to infuse. When the syrup is cold, remove the basil.

Place the apricots and cooled simple syrup in a blender and process until smooth.

To make the mimosas, pour the apricot purée a quarter of the way up a chilled champagne flute. Top up with the chilled champagne and serve.

CUCUMBER MARTINI

1 Persian cucumber, peeled
   and chopped
2 tablespoons simple syrup
   (see page 189)
6 mint leaves
1 tablespoon freshly squeezed
   lemon juice
ice cubes
¼ cup/60 ml vodka
fennel flowers, to decorate (optional)

SERVES 2

You may feel almost healthy (and a little less guilty) sipping on one of these, although there is nothing wrong with a dirty martini with blue cheese-stuffed olives at the end of a hard week either.

Place the cucumber, simple syrup, mint leaves, and lemon juice in a blender and process until smooth.

Fill a cocktail shaker with ice and pour in the cucumber mix, along with the vodka. Shake vigorously and pour into chilled glasses, then decorate with fennel flowers, if using.

BOBBIE'S FIZZ

24 kumquats, tops trimmed
2 cups/400 g granulated/caster sugar
1 tablespoon freshly squeezed
    lemon juice
pinch of sea salt
1 bottle of prosecco, chilled
edible flowers, to garnish (optional)

SERVES 6

This is such a wonderful way to finish a meal. Tangy kumquat sorbet floating in icy prosecco—it tastes even better than it looks. Serve in vintage coupe glasses for evening elegance and in small tumblers for a casual barbecue.

Place the kumquats in a medium-sized pan and cover with water. Bring to the boil over high heat, then drain. Repeat the procedure twice more—this will reduce the bitterness of the peel. Place the drained kumquats in a blender.

Bring the sugar and 2 cups/500 ml water to the boil in a pan over medium-high heat, stirring to dissolve the sugar. Reduce the heat to a simmer and cook for 5 minutes until the sugar has completely dissolved. Set aside to cool slightly.

Pour the sugar syrup into a blender with the kumquats and add the lemon juice and salt. Purée until smooth. Cover and set aside to cool, then refrigerate for 2 hours.

Freeze the mixture in an ice cream maker according to the manufacturer's instructions. Store in an airtight container in the freezer until ready to use.

To serve, add a scoop of sorbet to each glass and pour the prosecco over the top. Garnish with flowers, if using.

THE CAPRI

2 tangerines
¼ cup/60 ml Hendrick's gin
¼ cup/60 ml Campari
1 tablespoon freshly squeezed
  lemon juice
2 cups/450 g ice cubes
lavender sprigs, to garnish (optional)

SIMPLE SYRUP
1 cup/200 g white sugar

SERVES 4

Campari brings such a refreshing herbal tone to any cocktail and it doesn't disappoint here. You can use tangerines, oranges, kumquats, or mandarins in this cocktail—it's a fun way to drink round the year with whatever is in season.

To make the simple syrup, place the sugar and 1 cup/250 ml water in a saucepan and bring to the boil over medium-high heat. Reduce the heat and simmer until the sugar has dissolved. Remove from the heat and cool. This makes approx. 1 cup/250 ml. Store in a jar with a lid in the fridge.

Place the unpeeled tangerines, gin, Campari, lemon juice, and ¼ cup/60ml simple syrup in a blender along with the ice cubes. Process until smooth.

Pour into chilled glasses and garnish with lavender sprigs, if using.

WATERMELON MARGARITA

WITH TAJÍN-SALTED RIMS

2 tablespoons Chilerito Chamoy
  hot sauce
¼ teaspoon Tajín seasoning
1 tablespoon coarse sea salt
½ cup/120 ml tequila blanco
2 cups/300 g yellow watermelon
  chunks
small bunch of mint
¼ cup/60 ml simple syrup
  (see page 189)
2 cups/450 g crushed ice
grated zest and freshly squeezed
  juice of 1 lime

MAKES 2

Look out for the yellow watermelons with exotic names such as 'Moon and Stars' or 'Yellow Doll'. They look exactly the same as the pink-fleshed melons but are a little sweeter. They make the most gorgeous colored margaritas, especially when rimmed with Chilerito Chamoy hot sauce and Tajin-spiced salt.

Pour the hot sauce onto a small plate. On another small plate, mix together the Tajín and salt.

Dip the rims of the glasses first into the hot sauce, then into the salt mix and set aside.

Pour the tequila into a blender and add the watermelon, four sprigs of mint, simple syrup, ice, and lime zest and juice into a blender and process until smooth.

Pour into the salted glasses and garnish with a mint sprig.

SPICED ICED ALMOND HORCHATA FLOAT

1 cup/140 g raw almonds
2 tablespoons brown sugar
1 teaspoon ground cinnamon,
    plus extra to garnish
½ cup/125 ml dark rum
crushed ice
vanilla ice cream, or a flavor
    of your choice

SERVES 4

These floats are a really fun way to end a barbecue. They are refreshing and not too heavy, and can be served as a dessert. Make it for the kids too, but leave the rum out.

Soak the almonds in water for 6–24 hours.

Strain the almonds and place in a blender with 2 cups/500 ml water. Add the sugar, cinnamon, and rum and blend until smooth. Pour into a tall pitcher/jug filled with ice.

Fill four tall glasses with crushed ice and pour in the horchata, leaving a space of 1 inch/2.5 cm at the rim. Top with a scoop of ice cream and dust with a little cinnamon. Serve immediately.

INFUSED VODKAS

4 tangerines
2 lemons
fennel flowers
dried chiles/chillies
pink peppercorns
2 bottles of good-quality vodka

4 sterilized empty wine bottles

You can make infused vodkas and keep them in the freezer. They make a wonderful after-dinner digestif. You can flavor them with all sorts of fruits, herbs, and chiles/chillies, and as they sit in the freezer, the flavor intensifies. They are fun to bring to the table at the end of the meal when you are serving an ice-cold sorbet and let your guests choose a flavor to pour over. There are no rules with this recipe, except use good-quality vodka.

Slice the tangerines and lemons into pieces small enough to fit into the bottles.

This is where you get to have fun and mix and match the ingredients and place them in the bottles. You can use a mixture of tangerines and chiles/chillies, lemons with fennel flowers, or just use a single ingredient, such as pink peppercorns, for each bottle.

Once you have filled the bottles with the ingredients, top them up with the vodka, then seal. Place in the freezer until ready to use.

CHERRY VODKA MARTINI

crushed ice
1 cup/250 ml Cherry Vodka (see below)
¼ cup/60 ml dry vermouth
cherries, to garnish

SERVES 4

Martinis are the most glamorous of all cocktails. They are timeless, wonderfully sophisticated, and for many people a wonderful way to finish the day.

Fill a cocktail shaker with crushed ice. Pour in the Cherry Vodka and vermouth and shake for 30 seconds.

Place a cherry or two in each glass and pour in the martini.

COOKS' NOTE: If you want to serve the martinis on the rocks, fill the glasses with crushed ice before pouring over the cocktail.

CHERRY VODKA

3 cups/455 g ripe cherries, rinsed
3¼ cups/750 ml vodka

*a wide-mouthed sterilized glass jar
    with airtight lid*
*sterilized small bottles with
    airtight caps or flip lids*

MAKES 4½ CUPS/1 L

Another great way to enjoy cherries. Cherry vodka can be used in cocktails, poured over sorbets, or simply enjoyed as an after-dinner digestif.

Prick each cherry a few times with a wooden skewer or toothpick/ cocktail stick and place in a wide-mouthed sterilized glass jar.

Pour over the vodka and screw the lid on tightly. Store in a cool, dark place for at least 1 month before serving—the longer you leave the vodka the stronger the cherry flavor will become.

Decant into small bottles, seal and keep refrigerated for up to 12 months.

MEYER LIMONCELLO CHAMPAGNE COCKTAIL

Meyer Limoncello (see below), chilled
champagne, chilled, to top up

SERVES 6

Wonderful citrus Meyer Limoncello (see below) meets bubbles—a fun, refreshing drink to kick off cocktail hour. This is great served at parties as it is simple and fuss-free.

Pour a splash of Meyer Limoncello in the bottom of six chilled champagne glasses and top with the champagne. Serve at once.

MEYER LIMONCELLO

12 Meyer lemons
3¼ cups/750 ml vodka

SYRUP
1 cup/200 g granulated/caster sugar
1½ cups/350 ml water

a large sterilized glass jar
sterilized bottles with airtight lids

SERVES 6

Limoncello is a wonderful Italian citrus liqueur. It is simple to make at home and especially when fragrant Meyer lemons, in all their floral glory, show up at the market.

Peel the lemon skin with a sharp vegetable peeler, avoiding the pith. Squeeze the juice from the lemons into a large sterilized glass jar and add the peel. Pour in the vodka and stir. Cover and set aside at room temperature for 2 weeks.

To make the syrup, bring the sugar and water to the boil in a saucepan over medium-high heat. Reduce the heat and simmer for 10 minutes, stirring occasionally until the sugar has dissolved. Remove from the heat and allow to cool.

Add the syrup to the Limoncello mixture then set aside for 30 minutes.

Strain the liqueur though a cheesecloth/muslin or coffee filter into a pitcher/jug. Decant into sterilized bottles and label.

Store in the refrigerator or freezer for up to 12 months.

DARK & STORMY

crushed ice
1 cup/240 ml Goslings Black Seal rum
    or similar
Ginger Beer (see below), to top up
lime wedges, to serve

SERVES 4

Dark & Stormy is hailed as the national drink of Bermuda. Although its name sounds like trouble it is refreshing served over ice. Homemade ginger beer gives this drink a zestier flavor.

Fill four chilled glasses with crushed ice. Pour ¼ cup/60 ml of rum into each glass and top up with Ginger Beer.

Finish each glass with a squeeze of lime and serve.

OLD-FASHIONED GINGER BEER

2 x 4½-in/12-cm piece of fresh ginger,
    peeled and finely chopped
generous ¾ cups/175 g superfine/
    caster sugar
grated zest and juice of 1 lemon
1 teaspoon active dry yeast

*sterilized glass bottles with airtight caps
    or flip lids*

SERVES 4

The key to avoiding the bottles exploding is to screw the lids on loosely and keep checking throughout the 3-day fermentation that the ginger beer is not too fizzy; if it is, simply loosen the caps to release some of the bubbles.

Bring 5 cups/1.1 litres of water, the ginger and sugar to a boil in a saucepan over medium–high heat. Reduce the heat and simmer for 10 minutes, stirring occasionally until the sugar has dissolved. Remove from the heat and cool until the liquid is just warm.

Add the lemon zest, juice, and the yeast. Stir, and cover with a lid. Set aside in a warm place for at least 24 hours.

Strain the ginger beer through a cheesecloth/muslin or coffee filter into sterilized bottles. Loosely screw the caps on and set aside in a cool, dark place for 3 days before serving.

Store in the refrigerator for up to 4 days.

INDEX

ACKNOWLEDGMENTS

Summer rolled around and took us by the kind invitation of Todd Rubenstein to his ranch nestled in the rolling hills and farmland of Lompoc, California. Apple Creek Ranch sits between vineyards, a honey farm, and fields of organic produce as far as the eye can see. Thank you so much Todd for your gracious hospitality, taking us to feed the chickens, and letting me run into the fields at sunrise to harvest vegetables and flowers. The land is lovingly farmed by Andrew Gibson, of Sunrise Organics, who supplied all the vegetables, thank you. Erin Kunkel, thank you doesn't seem enough, you are so inspirational and shoot the most amazingly beautiful photographs. You did not put your camera down from dawn til dusk and the result is too heavenly for words. Gena Sigala, thank you so much for all that you touched. You brought style, beauty, and magic with all your props and styling. Thank you for hosting us and supplying our straw sun hats. A huge thank you goes to Connie Pikulas who tirelessly worked with me to cook up a storm and keep me straight! And for cooking our wrap dinner. Danny Hess, thank you for helping man the firepit and brewing iced coffee for our afternoon pick-me-up. Peter and Rebecca Work, of Ampelos Winery, Lompoc, for sharing their wonderful wines. As always, a huge thank you goes to Julia Charles and Leslie Harrington who asked me to write and style this book—it was a lot of fun being on location and cooking outside among the vines with the gentle ocean breezes coming over the hills. Lastly but not leastly, a huge thank you and love go to Martin, my husband who champions me every day.

ABOUT THE AUTHOR

Valerie Aikman-Smith is a Scottish food stylist, consultant, and cookbook author based in California. She has designed and styled food for award-winning movies and TV shows. She works internationally and has cooked in Greece, Paris, Mallorca, Mexico, Croatia, and Scotland, as well as the USA. Her work is seen in editorials, commercials, print, and advertising campaigns. She is the author of *Salt & Pepper, Smoke & Spice, Pickled & Packed, and Feast from the Fire* for Ryland Peters & Small. Check out www.valerieaikman-smith.com

ABOUT THE PHOTOGRAPHER

Erin Kunkel is an award-winning photographer and director who works around the globe. She spends her time in the foggy outer lands of San Francisco, and at her cabin in the Santa Cruz mountains. With deep roots in New York, Los Angeles, and Hawaii, she has contacts and crew at the ready. She and her husband spend their down time surfing, traveling, and entertaining friends at their rural getaway. Check out www.erin.kunkel.com